Glorious
BRITAIN

Glorious
BRITAIN

EDMUND SWINGLEHURST

WHSMITH

EXCLUSIVE
· BOOKS ·

Photographic acknowledgments

Aldeburgh Foundation 160; All-Sport 40–41, 51 bottom, 58–59, 60, 61, 62, 63, 64, 65, 66, 67, 84, 85, 96, 97, 98, 101, 102, 105, 107, 108–109, 110, 111; Catherine Ashmore 235; Bath International Festival 156; Belvoir Castle 55 top; John Bethell 55 bottom, 57, 71, 158–159, 167, 170–171, 188, 242; Brighton Arts Information Centre/Ian Sanderson 76–77, 78; Britain on View (BTA/ETB) 21, 22–23, 25 bottom, 30, 34–35, 81, 90–91, 100, 118, 171, 173 bottom; Dartmoor National Park 200–201; W. F. Davidson 130–131, 216 bottom, 250; Michael Dent 82; Derbyshire Countryside Limited 26; Zoë Dominic 234; Earls Court Exhibition Centre 241; East Midlands Tourist Board/Rodney Callow 10; English Wine Centre 193; Chris Fairclough 115; Alex Gillespie 185, 186; Godbolds 227; Guy Gravett 157; Great Yorkshire Show 119 top, 119 bottom; Hammonds Photography, Hereford 169; Brian Hawkes 202; The Heart of England Tourist Board 195; Marc Henrie 238–239, 240; HMS Heron 147; B. J. Holden 39; Holiday on Ice 229; Kit Houghton 43, 45, 51 top, 56, 146, 190–191; Jarrold & Sons Ltd 70; Geoff Johnson 87, 178; A. F. Kersting 52–53, 204–205; Bob Langrish 42, 44, 49, 225, 226; Sandra Langrish 192–193; Andrew Lawson 16–17, 20, 37 bottom; Moray District Council 246 right; The National Trust Photographic Library 205; Stuart Newsham 46–47; North Creake Photography 129 top; Northern Ireland Tourist Board 58, 136; Northumbria Tourist Board 134, 135; Photo Source 8, 86, 88–89, 92, 94–95, 211, 212, 217, 218 bottom, 220, 221, 242–243, 245; Royal Academy of Arts 83; Royal Tournament 148–149, 150–151; Ian Sanderson 74–75; Scottish Tourist Board 80, 152, 154, 161, 162, top, 162–163, 180, 182, 183 top, 237; Selfridges 231; Brian Shuel 6, 7, 11, 12, 13, 15, 18, 19, 25 top, 27, 28–29, 29, 30–31, 37 top, 72, 73, 99 top, 112, 113, 114, 129 bottom, 132, 137, 138, 139, 140, 141, 176, 179, 181, 194, 196, 197, 198, 199 top, 199 bottom, 210, 214, 215, 216 top, 218 top, 219, 228, 230, 232, 233, 236 top, 236 bottom, 246 left, 247, 249; Society of British Aerospace Companies 222–223; Deidre Sprott 9; The States of Jersey Tourist Board/Stuart Abraham 172, 173 top; Tait & McLay 183 bottom, 184; Taunton Cider/Circle Photography 206, 207; Tony Taylor 104–105; Peter Thornham 38; Judy Todd 14, 48, 52 top, 68–69, 115, 120, 121, 124, 155; Topham Picture Library 116–117; TPS Public Relations 238; TRH Pictures 99 bottom; TRH Pictures/Mike Roberts 143; TSW, Plymouth 203; Wellington Enterprises 127 top, 127 bottom; Welsh Tourist Board 122, 122–123, 164, 165, 166, 186–187, 208, 209; C. F. D. Whetmath 40; York Archaeological Trust 248; ZEFA Picture Library (UK) Limited 103, 125, 126, 133, 174–175.

Titlespread: Henley Regatta (J. Allan Cash Ltd)
Endpapers: Trooping the Colour (Tony Stone)

This edition produced exclusively for
W H Smith

Published by
The Hamlyn Publishing Group
Bridge House, London Road, Twickenham, Middlesex TW1 3SB

Copyright © The Hamlyn Publishing Group Limited 1987
ISBN 0 600 50395 X

Printed in Spain

Contents

Introduction	**6**
The Rites of Spring	**14**
Springtime Pageantry	16
May Day and Other Springtime Rituals	28
Throwing Off Winter's Traces	41
Epic Struggles	59
The Gentle Side of Spring	68
Summer Is 'Icumen' In	**80**
The Beginning of the Season	82
The Royal Summer	87
Gentlemen and Players	103
Summer in the Country	112
The Military Shows	142
Festival Time	153
Summer By the Sea	172
Season of Mists and Mellow Fruitfulness	**178**
Sporting Autumn	180
Last of the Summer Wine	192
In the Countryside	196
Crinolines and Motorized Carriages	207
Pageantry and Plots	211
The End of Autumn	224
A Winter of Delights	**228**
Show Time	233
The Big Exhibitions	239
Ancient Traditions of Winter	243
Viking Winter	247
Chinese New Year	249
Calendar of Events	**251**
Index	**252**

Introduction

Knutsford's Royal May Day Festival is the largest of the traditional May Day celebrations and includes processions, morris dancers, a Jack o' the Green and unique street decorations in coloured sand.

The Duc de Sully, adviser to Henry IV of France, once remarked that the English took their pleasures sadly. Like most generalizations, this was wide of the mark, for Sully was drawing conclusions from a visit to England when the Puritan spirit of Cromwell was the order of the day; on the whole, British history does not bear him out. There have been times, during the reigns of Mary Tudor, Oliver Cromwell and Victoria, when glumness seems to have been the national mood, but the records and existing traditions suggest that the British have a capacity for enjoyment equal to any other nation.

In Tudor times, pageantry, sport and merrymaking were widespread and the spirit of optimism which pervades the works of Shakespeare and other writers of the time prevailed. This feeling was exemplified by Bankside, on the south side of the Thames in London where theatrical entertainment, bear baiting, brothels and other diversions flourished.

During the reign of Charles II there was the same spirit of enjoyment, and it survived into the 18th century, when the fireworks, music and other entertainments in pleasure gardens like Vauxhall and Ranelagh provided for city dwellers what markets and fairs did for the rural population.

The 19th century is remembered for the high moral tone of its latter years, when Britain was concerned about its world image as an imperial power. However, it was also a period of national exuberance – though in a more restrained style than earlier years. In fact, many of the pageants, military and royal occasions, sporting events and other celebrations which we still enjoy today date from this era.

Today, Britain, having shed its role of a paternalistic world power, has regained some of its *joie de vivre*. Profiting from a long history of traditions, Britain puts on an all-the-year-round show which delights the radical as well as the traditionalist and reveals aspects of the British character not visible through recorded reports. The events that fill the British calendar are many and varied, and the magnificent settings, which range from stately city buildings to castles, from a countryside of fields and hedgerows to wild mountains and lakes, enhance the experience. The visitor to a festival or sporting meeting can enjoy not only the event itself, but the buildings and landscape in the vicinity.

The celebratory aspects of British life often have a fascinating history. Some, like the Cheese Rolling ceremonies at Randwick or the Hobby Horse festivities at Padstow, can trace their origins to pagan times. Others, like the Pancake Race at Olney or the Royal Maundy ceremony, are rooted in early Christian tradition. Some festivals celebrate great events in

A huge Easter Parade takes place at Battersea Park in London where scores of decorated floats, dancers, bands and costumed paraders enliven Easter Sunday.

national history, like the Garter Ceremony at Windsor or the Viking Festival at Lerwick; others commemorate great national figures, like Shakespeare at Stratford-upon-Avon or Robbie Burns at Ayr.

There are, of course, the great sporting events – often more than just a competition, having something of the atmosphere of old-time fairs. Predominant in the spring are the equestrian contests, ranging from jousting tournaments to three-day events. There are steeplechases, which originated as ancient tests of horsemanship for mounted soldiers, and flat races like the Derby, which were created to gratify the landed gentry's compulsion to gamble. Today, the celebrations of equestrian skill and courage are countless, providing every section of society with the colour and excitement that is characteristic of race meetings.

An unusual event which takes place in Northern Ireland on St. Patrick's Day is the All Horse Plough Match at Fairhead, a fine headland above the sea near Ballycastle. In an age where the motor car rules, this day devoted to an ancient skill is rewarding indeed.

On the day of the contest the chosen site for the competition is thronged from the early hours with farmers and spectators as the great Clydesdale horses are prepared for the match and their harnesses are polished and rubbed until they shine. As it is March the weather is sometimes cool and the refreshment tents are kept busy serving coffee and tea and a tot or two of Irish whiskey.

The ploughing competition is in four main categories: Swing, Whole Work, Everyday and Broken ploughing, according to the type of plough and nature of the work to be done. Each category has its own judges, expert in their particular skill, and the performance of horse and ploughman is also watched critically by the spectators, many of whom also know a thing or two about the finer points of ploughing.

Above: Not a tractor in sight! The All Horse Plough Match at Fairhead has been held for over 100 years in this beautiful region of Ulster.

Opposite: The sporting events of springtime include a re-enactment of medieval jousts and tournaments. This galloping knight is taking part in the medieval fair at Cuckmere Valley, Sussex.

Spring flowers are the basis of the colourful and beautifully decorated floats at the Flower Festival at Spalding, Lincolnshire, the centre of the flower bulb industry.

Apart from the main ploughing match there are other competitions, one for ladies' ploughing and another for the turn-out of horse and ploughman. This simple event, rare in the motorized world of today, is much appreciated by those who enjoy the glorious sight of horse and ploughman as they perform one of the oldest skills in agriculture.

The renowned British love of animals is also the source of numerous other events which take place either out of doors, such as sheepdog trials, or indoors in large exhibition halls, which are filled at certain times of the year with champion dogs, champion cats and even champion cage birds.

Working dogs also go through their paces at the many country fairs which provide a meeting place for those engaged in the business of agriculture. Here is an opportunity for everyone to watch show jumping, hound and sheepdog displays, fly casting competitions, clay pigeon shooting and many other country pastimes. A more domestic side of country life is represented at the flower shows that are staged throughout Britain in spring and summer. The most prestigious of these is London's Chelsea Flower Show which takes place in the grounds of the Royal Hospital. Another important flower festival is held at Spalding in Lincolnshire and is devoted to the celebration of the many varieties of spring flowers which decorate the colourful floats in the procession.

Sporting events abound in the British calendar, particularly in the first half of the year, when the football and rugby seasons come to a climax with the F.A. Cup Final and the closing stages of the rugby championship between England, Scotland, Wales, Ireland and France. Both of these sports began in the Middle Ages, acquiring, over the years, rules of play. The spread of both football and rugby throughout the world took place during the 19th century due to British influence, and football is now the world's most popular game. Cup Final Day generates enormous excitement throughout the country and is a festive as well as an extremely partisan occasion.

Another major sporting highlight of the year is the Oxford v. Cambridge University Boat Race, in itself only a small event in the world of rowing but one that has caught the public imagination, attracting thousands of spectators to the banks of the River Thames on Boat Race Day. The enthusiasm for regattas continues throughout the summer and peaks at the Henley Royal Regatta, when the river banks of this ancient Thames-side town are thronged with spectators and ring with the sound of fairground entertainments.

The uniquely English sport of cricket also provides a holiday atmosphere at Test match series between England and Australia, India,

Pakistan, New Zealand, Sri Lanka and the West Indies. The series are played, among other places, at the grounds of Old Trafford, Manchester; Headingly, Leeds; the Oval, Kennington and at the hallowed ground of Lords – home of the Marylebone Cricket Club.

'Anyone for tennis?' The answer to this question, once a Wodehousian joke, is that today everyone is! Wimbledon fortnight, once a purely English affair, now attracts players and spectators from all over the world and is one of the major attractions of the British summer calendar.

The sporting celebrations of the British year are counterbalanced by cultural festivals and fairs throughout the country. Many festivals derive from charters granted to medieval lords of the manor. At the Nottingham Goose Fair or at Tavistock Fair some of the atmosphere of the past exists – though today there are more trucks and vans than horse-drawn wagons!

A multitude of cultural festivals are held each year, celebrating the arts of painting, sculpture, music, folk dancing, singing and bagpiping. The season of art festivals begins with the opening of the Royal Academy Summer Exhibition at which some 1500 works by British painters, sculptors, engravers and draughtsmen are exhibited. This is followed by such world-famous events as the Edinburgh Festival, the Three Choirs Festival and summer opera and music seasons at Glyndebourne and Aldeburgh.

As well as the grander elements of the British year, there are many others of a more local nature which also carry on historic traditions and customs. These are a source of great enjoyment and celebration, helping to complete the picture of the lighter side of British life. Among these are the Dunmow Flitch ceremony, where a side of bacon is presented to the married couple who have managed to live through the year without a cross word, the unique Abbotts Bromley Horn Dance, which celebrates the hunting of deer in medieval times, the Rush-bearing Festivals at Ambleside and Grasmere, and the Furry Dance at Helston in Cornwall.

The Abbots Bromley Horn Dance, which takes place in Staffordshire, is an ancient autumn ritual which may date back to before the arrival of William the Conqueror.

This book gives examples of festivals from all parts of Britain, featuring all the great ceremonies and at least one example of other types of event. Time is taken to describe the countryside in which the event takes place, for it is often the life, work and history of the region which has given rise to particular celebrations.

There has not been enough space to include all the events that add colour and excitement to the British year, but it is hoped that this record of some hundred celebrations and festivals gives a picture of the rich, varied and joyful pattern of events that make up the year in glorious Britain.

The rushes that once covered stone flagged floors give rise to a semi-religious festival of rush-bearing to the local church. In Grasmere, Cumbria, this takes place in August.

The Rites of Spring

A bright yellow carpet of daffodils welcomes the spring in the gardens of the Fitzwilliam Museum, Cambridge.

Springtime in Britain is a season of natural drama which has inspired generations of British poets. To Chaucer it was the season of sweet showers when birds made music and nature inspired people to go on pilgrimages. Shakespeare expressed the exuberance of spring in his song 'It was a lover and his lass, with a hey and a ho and a hey nonny no, that over the green fields did go, in spring time, in spring time, the only pretty ring time.' This concept was echoed by Tennyson when he wrote: 'In spring a young man's fancy lightly turns to thoughts of love.' Swinburne, however, dwelt on the emerging beauty of nature when he described how 'In green underwood and cover, blossom by blossom the spring begins.' More recently, T. S. Eliot expressed a more bitter truth about spring: 'April is the cruellest month, breeding lilacs out of the dead land, mixing memory and desire.'

Britain is fortunate in its spring. It unfolds like a well-constructed drama full of joyful surprises – the sudden shafts of sunlight after a shower of rain, the sight of crocuses glowing under the trees in a park. Those who have gardens look anxiously for the first signs of spring flowers planted before winter began. The British spring arrives slowly, almost ceremonially, with one event following another in quiet succession. The crocuses burst out of the ground, followed by the daffodils that gladdened the heart of Wordsworth. In the hedgerows, primroses, wild orchids and may blossom abound. The migratory birds arrive and the trees deck themselves in a fresh translucent green, filling out and deepening in colour as summer approaches. And the people join in the celebration of the rebirth of natural life; the countryman goes about his seasonal duties – mending and replanting hedgerows, watching young lambs, planting out the vegetable garden and sowing wheat, while the city dwellers set out their windowboxes and discard their winter coats.

In ancient times the arrival of spring reassured mankind. It was a sign that life would return to the land, crops would grow and existence was assured. The people therefore celebrated this regeneration with sacrificial ceremonies designed to propitiate and thank the gods, and with festivals, competitions and games which released their new found energy. Today, despite the scientists' explanations for what were once natural mysteries, the magic of spring persists and man continues to celebrate with events which range over every aspect of British life. These events include royal occasions, military ceremonies, sporting events, traditional customs and shows of various kinds including, of course, flower shows.

Because of its long history and rich and varied heritage, Britain has a remarkable range of springtime celebrations which together provide a colourful introduction to the people and to the events that will fill the rest of their year.

The Easter Parade at Battersea Park on the south bank of the River Thames is a dazzling jamboree of processions and entertainments which includes guest participants from overseas.

15

SPRINGTIME PAGEANTRY

It sometimes surprises the visitor to discover that while he is all agog to see a member of the Royal Family drive past, or to catch a glimpse of mounted Horse Guards exercising in Hyde Park, citizens of the capital will walk on, apparently untouched by the presence of the human symbols of Britain's traditions and history. Appearances are deceptive, however, and given the right occasion the British crowds are not lacking in enthusiasm. You see them on city pavements and village squares, at race meetings and on cathedral steps, waving a Union Jack, calling 'God Bless you Ma'am' in an involuntary outburst of national pride or, in the case of the stiff upper lip brigade, standing tautly and craning their necks to follow the object of their admiration.

Despite the occasional sneer by republican-minded columnists, royal occasions and pageantry are not empty gestures but a projection of deep national feeling which most people would be embarrassed to declare openly. If this were not the case, the tide of emotion that sweeps a crowd as the Guards arrive to take their posts at Buckingham Palace or that more heightened feeling as the Queen is driven up the Mall on her return from Trooping the Colour, would not exist.

Royal occasions take place throughout the year but the atmosphere of spring makes them especially memorable. The first royal ceremony of spring is a reminder of the gentle side of medieval royal power. This is the Royal Maundy, a ritual derived from an incident after the Last Supper

when Jesus washed the feet of his disciples in turn, commanding them to love one another.

In Britain this symbolic act of humility and penance was adopted by the monarchs Edward I, II and III, who personally participated in the ceremony of washing the feet of the poor and distributing gifts of food, clothing and money. Unlike other Christian countries, where Maundy charity is extended to only 12 people representing the 12 disciples, in Britain the Royal Maundy involves as many people as the reigning monarch has years. In 1363, for example, there were 50 recipients of the Maundy money for Edward III's fiftieth birthday. The practice of feet washing came to be performed by servants of the monarch, later to be dropped altogether. James II was probably the last king to participate in this ceremony.

Today only Maundy money is distributed but certain symbolic aspects of the original Maundy ceremony remain. The nosegays of flowers represent those which used to be carried to counteract infection and the odour of unwashed feet, and the towels worn by the Lord High Almoner and his assistants, which resemble large white sheets, are a reminder of the days when similarly placed officials gave a preliminary ablution to the feet which the Sovereign was to wash later.

From 1890 until 1952 the Royal Maundy service was held in Westminster Abbey, then from 1952 to 1970 on alternate years in the Abbey and in other cathedrals in Britain. Now the Abbey is seldom used,

The Life Guards are a colourful feature of many of the royal events of the British calendar. They exercise their horses in Hyde Park, and here are returning to Buckingham Palace through Wellington Arch.

Above: On Maundy Thursday the Queen distributes the Royal Maundy at one of Britain's great cathedrals. In this picture Her Majesty is emerging from the door of Southwell Cathedral flanked by a bodyguard of Yeomen of the Guard.

Opposite: The recipients of the Royal Maundy are presented with two purses containing coins, a red one with money in lieu of the clothing once given by the monarch and a white one with specially minted coins whose value represents the Sovereign's age.

the last service being held there in 1981 and the next service expected to be in 1991. In 1987 Ely cathedral was the venue for the Royal Maundy.

It is an impressive occasion. The procession consists of over one hundred people: choristers and musicians precede the cathedral clergy up the nave of the cathedral. Then follow the Head Verger, the Dean or Provost, the Queen and Prince Philip, Her Majesty's Suite and the Lord Lieutenant of the County. Lastly comes the Royal Almonry Procession, which includes the Yeomen of the Guard – the Queen's Bodyguard – officials of the Royal Almonry and the Lord High Almoner. During a pause in the service, the Queen distributes the Maundy Money, first to the women and then to the men. The simple but moving ceremony ends with a prayer and the national anthem.

Another royal ceremony is the Changing of the Guard at Buckingham Palace. Though this takes place every day throughout the year, there is little doubt that spring and summertime are the seasons when it is most rewarding to watch, for when winter greatcoats are shed the Guards' uniforms are at their most resplendent and St. James's Park, with its lovely lake and fine plane trees, is at its best.

Guard duty at the palace is shared by a number of regiments; their brilliant red tunics and imposing bearskins give an especially exotic touch to the proceedings. The Buckingham Palace guard duty coincides with that of guarding St. James's Palace which, though not now inhabited by the monarch, is still the official residence of the Court and the place to which foreign ambassadors are appointed. There are, therefore, two guard changes to be made every day.

Proceedings begin at 11 a.m. as the St. James's Palace detachment of the Old Guard gathers in Friary Court and then marches to the forecourt of Buckingham Palace to join the Old Guard of the Palace. Meanwhile, the

New Guard forms up in the forecourt of the barracks at Bird Cage Walk, which runs alongside St. James's Park, and then marches to the Palace.

During the ceremony a military band plays in the forecourt of the Palace and eager crowds line the railings and climb on to the steps of the Queen Victoria Memorial which stands in front of the Palace. Cameras click, mounted policemen keep an eye on the crowds and the traffic and, if the Sovereign is at home, the Royal Standard flaps lazily in the breeze above the Palace.

The Palace keys are handed over to the New Guard and the new sentries are posted, with much stamping of feet and saluting, while the band continues to play. It is a familiar scene for many – but it never loses its magic. After the ceremony the band plays the Old Guards back to the barracks and the detachment of New Guards for St. James's Palace marches off with its Colour to take up its own guard duty.

Buckingham Palace and St. James's Palace are not the only places to have a ceremonial guard change. A guard is also mounted at the charming building of the Horse Guards, which was designed by William Kent and stands on a part of the site of the old Whitehall Palace. Guard changes also take place at the Tower of London and at Windsor Castle.

The Civil War, one of the most romantic (and traumatic) periods of English history, which ended with the shocking execution of a king, is re-enacted at various locations throughout the spring and summer by Roundheads, followers of Oliver Cromwell, and Cavaliers, loyal supporters of King Charles I.

The Sealed Knot Society, made up of some 5000 members who provide their own dress and accoutrements for the battles they re-enact, was founded in 1969 by Brigadier Peter Young. Today the society has all the

Above: The Household Cavalry. Changing the guard at Horse Guards, Whitehall, evokes a romantic image of Britain's military past.

Opposite: The Changing of the Guard at Buckingham Palace never ceases to attract a large public from all over the world. A Guards band plays as the guards take up their posts.

The Sealed Knot, a society of enthusiastic students of military history, recreate one of the battles between Cavaliers and Roundheads near Warwick Castle.

23

authentic-looking equipment for its appearances, usually in aid of charity, at events throughout Britain, and occasionally even abroad. Among its weaponry there are cannons, muskets, swords, halberds and pikes and the costumes are careful replicas, often made by the members themselves. Though the venues change from year to year, the Society puts in a regular appearance at Stratton in Cornwall, a Royalist county. Stratton is inland from the popular seaside resort of Bude and is the site of a battle fought in 1643.

The careful preparation and attention to detail by the members of the Sealed Knot ensures that the battles have an authentic atmosphere and evoke a colourful era in English history. In October, at the end of their season of appearances, the Sealed Knot meet for a church service at Edge Hill, scene of a battle between the army of Charles I and Cromwell. This is a symbolic gesture of peacemaking for a struggle which, in the 17th century, changed the course of English history.

SHROVETIDE AND EASTER

The 40 days between Shrove Tuesday and Easter Sunday, though essentially a period of Christian observance, are a curious mixture of pagan practices and Christian ethic. Shrove Tuesday, or Mardi Gras as it is called in other countries, is the final burst of self-indulgence before the sacrifices and abstentions of Lent. Even today, the day before Lent still shows its pagan origins in curious ceremonies concerned with eating, playing violent competitive games and watching entertainments such as wrestling and horse-racing. The eating ritual probably originates in the need to consume all the foods that were to be renounced over Lent and the games, especially football, may be related to animal sacrifices at which the head of the beast was passed or kicked from person to person.

The main ceremonial of Easter is, however, based on Christian observance and this comes to a high point over the Easter weekend beginning with Maundy Thursday and ending with the joyous festival of Easter Sunday when the old pagan festival of the rebirth of the sun and the coming of spring is transformed into the Christian festival of the Resurrection.

Easter Sunday, in particular, is a big event in every cathedral and parish church in Britain, and they are beautifully decorated with flowers for the occasion. Few churches are empty on Easter Sunday, which vies with Christmas as an event not only of Christian ethic but of a deeply felt need to acknowledge the significance of this period of the year. The grandest of the Easter celebrations are in the great cathedrals of Britain and are presided over by the highest clergy in the land, with the Dean of Westminster officiating at Westminster Abbey and the Catholic Archbishop at Westminster Cathedral.

In these great churches of the Anglican and Catholic faith the observance of Easter Sunday is an impressive and moving spectacle. The wonderful buildings, the impressively robed clergy, the well trained choirs and the resounding organs all conspire to create an atmosphere in which the congregations take part as if in some great drama of national as well as spiritual life.

Although the great ceremonies in the cathedrals of Britain are the high point of Easter celebrations, they are not the only ones to be observed in the period between Shrove Tuesday and Easter Sunday. In many parts of the country other ancient rituals are performed, some dating back to Celtic times and others from even earlier.

The first of the traditional events to take place is the famous Pancake Race at Olney, Buckinghamshire. This particular ritual is inspired by the Christian calendar and takes place on Shrove Tuesday, the day of

Above: The Shrovetide football game at Alnwick, Northumberland, is more organized than most of these ancient scrimmages. Here is an action picture around the decorated goal with the castle in the background.

Left: The ladies at Olney, Buckinghamshire, wear the regulation headscarf and apron as they race towards the finishing line at the Olney Pancake Race.

repentance before the beginning of Lent. According to legend, it began when a housewife was trying to use up some of the ingredients which were not permitted during the Lenten fast – eggs, butter and flour – by making pancakes. Her cooking was interrupted by the sound of the church bell calling parishioners to the service of repentance and forgiveness – Shriving. Anxious not to arrive late, the good lady ran out of her house and down the High Street frying pan in hand, and thus created a tradition which has continued for more than 500 years.

Today her example is followed by the housewives of Olney, who run with their pans and pancakes over a distance of 379.5 m (415 yds) to the church. All ladies must wear an apron and headscarf and the pancake must be tossed three times before the contestant crosses the finishing line. The race is an excuse for a village festival which attracts many visitors. Ladies rush down the High Street, television cameras turn, crowds cheer and the winning lady receives a kiss from the bellringer and a prayer book from the Vicar. Afterwards a good lunch can be enjoyed in local hostelries with, of course, pancakes for dessert.

A more boisterous pancake competition takes place at Westminster School, London, where boys of the Great and Under Schools struggle for pieces of a pancake tossed over a bar by the school chef. At one time the Pancake Greaze, as it is called, involved any number of boys who wished to take part and not only the pancake but also the boys' clothes were torn to shreds. These days the Pancake Greaze is a more regulated affair with only 15 boys to each of the two teams. Even so, there is considerable wear and tear on both the boys and their clothes before those who have been determined or lucky enough present their piece of captured pancake and are given a money prize for their efforts.

Up'ards and Down'ards, people born on the north or south side of Henmore Brook, at Ashbourne, Derbyshire, struggle for possession of a ball with which they will score in goals three miles apart.

Another Shrove Tuesday custom which still persists is that of kicking a ball over a chosen piece of countryside or through streets with goals which can be several miles apart, though usually about a mile. The match can last for two days. This free-for-all game of football, which is performed at Ashbourne in Derbyshire, Sedgefield in County Durham and Alnwick in Northumberland, bears little resemblance to the football played in the stadiums. It is thought that it may have originated from the ancient custom of kicking the head of a sacrificial animal in order to gain some of the good fortune that it was hoped the sacrifice would bring to those who performed it.

At Hallaton, Leicestershire, beer barrels are used instead of a ball and the event is accompanied by another ceremony involving a hare pie. It seems likely that the Hare Pie Scramble dates back to pre-Christian times, when hares were considered sacred animals, protected by the goddess of the woods. The ceremony takes place on Easter Monday and begins with a service at the local church where the hare pies are blessed. The pies are then cut into portions which are tossed to the participants, who scramble to grab a piece. After the scramble and lunch there is a gathering of participants and spectators at the barrel-kicking contest. This takes place over a 1-mile stretch of open ground between two rivers. There are two teams and anyone can join in. Each team endeavours to kick two out of three barrels, one of which is empty, across his own line. This 'own goal' earns the winning team the right to consume the contents of the full barrels! Like the Shrove Tuesday football games, the barrel-kicking is a last vestige of pagan sacrificial ritual.

Hares and rabbits have long been a part of the Easter scene, as have eggs, which are considered to be symbols of creation. Egg rituals persist

The Hare Pie at Hallaton, Leicestershire, is carried through the streets to be blessed and cut by the rector before being scrambled for by young contestants.

Midgely, a small village in West Yorkshire, is the scene of an unusual Pace (Passover) Egg Play on Good Friday. The actors are pupils of the Calder Valley High School.

not only in the customary Easter Egg gifts but also as elements in some strange and inexplicable customs.

At Preston, a large industrial town in Lancashire, the custom of Pace Egg rolling takes place on Easter Monday. The word 'pace' comes from Passover, referring to the Judaic feast. However, it is likely that the egg rolling ritual has older and more mysterious origins. Children arrive at Avenham Park, Preston, with bags or baskets of brightly painted hard-boiled eggs, and nowadays chocolate eggs too, and line up along the slopes. The eggs are rolled to the accompaniment of cheers from their parents and onlookers. A similar ritual takes place at Scarborough, that delightful resort on the North Yorkshire coast.

MAY DAY AND OTHER SPRING RITUALS

The Easter period of rituals and celebrations are not long before May Day, a more pagan acknowledgment of the time of nature's rebirth. The celebration of May Day began long before the May Day holiday was established, and its origins are undoubtedly in such pre-Christian fertility rites as the erecting of the Maypole, a symbolic representation of a tree, the king of plant creation, and also a phallic symbol.

Another aspect of the traditional May Day celebrations that suggests that they were originally rituals of virility and youthful exuberance is the presence of the morris dancers, who put in an appearance in spring and continue to dance at village festivals throughout the summer. The exclusively masculine morris dancers with their colourful costumes, staves and swords are descendants of the troops of dancers of Tudor times, and even earlier, who toured the countryside as promoters of fertility and protectors of the harvest. These dancers were often accompanied by other characters which included the hobby horse, the fool and the Betty – a man

Overleaf: The Abingdon Morris Men welcome in May Morning in Oxford, where it has long been a popular tradition for morris dancing to be performed in the city centre on this special day.

The maypole is an essential element of spring rituals though today few adults take part in the Maypole Dance, except at Ickwell, Bedfordshire, where they perform the complex dance seen here.

dressed as a woman, representing a witch of either good or evil character.

Today, such auxiliary personages are not often part of a morris dancing team but make their appearance alone, as in the Padstow May Day festival. This festival, thought to be Celtic in origin, is one of the most mysterious of all the surviving regional ceremonies. The main characters in the May Day celebrations are two hobby horses. The first Hobby Horse is a strange cylindrical figure, draped in black, with a horse's tail. It has two heads – a horse's head and the grotesque head of a monster with a beak and a red tongue. The monster's head is black, covered with tufts of white hair and has the look of an African sculpture. The second character is another Hobby Horse, but it carries a blue ribbon instead of the red one worn by the first horse. Both horses have a companion known as the Teaser. He carries a spade-like instrument, called the club, with which he teases and intimidates the horse, obliging it to do a dance. To provide musical accompaniment there is a group of singers and musicians called the Doom Bar Pirates (Doom Bar being the dangerous sandbank across the mouth of the river Camel, on which Padstow is situated).

The day begins when the Hobby Horses emerge from the Gold Lion Pub

and begin their tour of the town. They are accompanied by the crowds who gather to watch the antics as the horses visit the village houses to wish the occupants good luck and happiness. The crowds also participate in the ritual by teasing the horses and encouraging them to charge, thereby bringing good luck. In ancient days the horses carried a tar brush with which it marked young women, transferring to them the power to bring fertility to nature.

Throughout the day the horses' journey around the pretty fishing village of Padstow is punctuated by a melancholy song, known as the Day Song, which runs:

Oh where is St. George?
Oh where is he Oh?
He's down in his long boat all on the salt sea Oh,
Up flies the kite and down flies the lark Oh.
There was an old woman and she had an old ewe,
And she died in her own park Oh.

No one knows what the song means, but it appears to have some potency. It casts its spell on the crowds who grow silent until it is ended.

At Padstow, Cornwall, the Old 'Oss, distinguished by a red ribbon, and the newer or Blue Ribbon 'Oss dance round the town on May Day in a ritual with a pagan character.

33

At the end of the day the Hobby Horses appear to have become exhausted and fall to the ground, attended by the Teaser. Just as they seem to be on the point of death, they revive, rise to the accompaniment of the Night Song and continue to caper long into the night.

As well as the Hobby Horses, the Cornish coast around Padstow offers its own festival of spring with a display of wild flowers on its rugged cliffs and the budding trees in its valleys, encouraged by the warm south-west breezes. This is a magical part of Cornwall with memories of King Arthur and his knights on the River Camel at Camelford, believed by some to be the legendary Camelot. On the coast lies Tintagel, with the so-called King Arthur's Castle set on a crag over Merlin's Cave. Whether or not the

legend is true seems hardly to matter; the setting is so perfect for Arthurian legends, with the rugged cliffs and rolling seas of the north Cornish coast.

The south of Cornwall has its own traditional May festival at Helston, where the whole town celebrates the arrival of spring with the Furry Dance. The meaning of the word 'furry' is lost in the mists of time, but some say that it stands for floral and others that it comes from the old Celtic word for fair. Today, the Furry Dance is associated with St. Michael who fought the Devil at Helston when he was carrying a stone brought from the mouth of hell. The Devil was defeated and dropped the stone in the town, hence the name Helston. Whatever the significance of the Furry Dance, there is no doubt about the enthusiasm of the local inhabitants for this spring festival. It is declared a local holiday except, of course, for the pubs, cafés and restaurants that satisfy thousands of thirsty dancers and visitors throughout the day.

The day starts with the young people of Helston going out into the surrounding countryside to collect spring flowers and leaves, bringing spring into the town where dancing can break out as early as 7 a.m. During the morning there is a special children's dance and at midday the adult citizens, including dignitaries of the town dressed in top hats and tails, join in, accompanied by the music of the town's band. Between the dances there are other entertainments, including a mumming play in which characters called Robin Hood, St. George, the Spaniards and Aunt Mary Moses make their appearance to the accompaniment of the 'Hal an Tow' song, the last verse of which runs:

And we were up as soon as any day Oh,
And for to fetch the summer home,
The summer and the May Oh,
For summer is a come Oh,
And winter is a go Oh,
With Hal an Tow,
Jolly Rumble Oh.

The dancers wend their way through the streets of Helston, going in and out of houses whose doors are left open. The streets are lined with stalls and there is a fairground outside the town where a good time is had by all.

Helston is a pretty town, originally one of the stannary towns from which the Cornish tin industry was regulated. It lies near the Loe Pool which, like Dozmary Pool on Bodmin Moor, claims to be the place associated with the sword Excalibur. To north and south sweeps the huge bay in the Cornish pincer between Lands End and the Lizard – a most spectacular area full of small fishing villages and great stretches of sandy beach at Penzance and Praa Sands.

Many of the traditional celebrations of Britain continue to exist in various towns and villages throughout the country – often in different forms. The veneration of water sources is an example of this phenomenon. In the ages before easily available tap water, the source of their water was of supreme importance to all human communities. Wells, springs, streams and fountains were all revered and in Roman times even had their own god, Pontus, who was propitiated at certain times to ensure that he kept the water flowing.

In Britain, the veneration of water supplies took various forms; in Scotland they tied pieces of cloth on the branches of trees and bushes around the source, in other places people threw coins into the water, as they still do today. In some places wells were decorated with flowers in an elaborate manner and this tradition has been maintained in places such as Bisley near Stroud and also at Tissington and many other places in Derbyshire and Staffordshire.

One of the earliest well dressings of the year takes place at Burton-upon-Trent, a famous brewery town where the well-dressing ritual is combined with May Day celebrations. The day begins with a procession to a well which is blessed and after this the May Day celebrations begin with a fair and numerous sporting events and entertainments.

Often the beautiful and painstaking decoration of a well is considered an event in itself and the wonderful Biblical scenes, entirely made from flowers and leaves at Youlgreave, Tideswell and Wirksworth, are proof enough of this.

Springtime high spirits and laughter are expressed at the International Clowns Convention at Bognor Regis on the West Sussex coast, for this is the gathering place of clowns from all over the world in April. There are

Left: Flowers feature in many springtime ceremonies. At Abbotsbury, Dorset, where a famous abbey once stood, children visit the village houses to extract money for their garlands – one of wild the other of cultivated flowers.

Below: The old custom of well dressing still persists in many villages in Britain. This gaily decorated well is at Tissington, Derbyshire, where the tradition of well dressing has been carried on for centuries.

traditional clowns with big flat feet and red noses and tramp-style clowns with their ragged clothes and woebegone expressions, elegant clowns with white faces and sequined costumes, large clowns on stilts and little clowns, fat clowns and thin clowns, and they all gather in Bognor to entertain visitors from Britain and many parts of the world.

The focus of the clown convention is the Gala Show, where there is the largest gathering of laughter-makers in the world. There is also a grand clown procession in which anyone is allowed to join if properly attired. There are street fairs, shops, clown displays and everything is geared to the idea of clowns and circuses, including a grand firework display by the sea which gives a final touch of Big Top dazzle and glitter to a celebration of one of the most heartening of human qualities – clowning.

There are many steam festivals in Britain during the spring and summer. Enthusiasts who have formed societies to preserve the superb engines and carriages of the days of the steam railways light up the boilers of their beautifully maintained engines and show the world what the romance of railways is about.

There are more than 500 societies dedicated to the preservation of engines and rolling stock and more than 1000 miles of track are used to demonstrate or to organize trips on steam trains and thus to provide a nostalgic glimpse of times gone by.

Clowns from all over the world mingle with the crowds during a fun-filled weekend at Bognor Regis where the annual International Clowns Convention is held.

Some of the steam railways like the Bluebell Line, the Watercress Line in Hampshire and the narrow gauge Welsh railways, such as Ffestiniog and Rheidol are well known; others, perhaps less well known, nevertheless preserve aspects of steam railway history which are a precious part of the British heritage. One of these is the Didcot Railway Centre in Berkshire, which operates on a line made famous by one of the world's most ingenious and prolific inventors, Isambard Kingdom Brunel.

Brunel was the creator of the Great Western Railway broad gauge system as well as the designer of the *Great Eastern*, the world's largest steam ship in its time and the *Great Britain*, the first screw driven steam ship, now at Bristol. The line that Brunel built was designed to reach the west of England ports from which ships sailed to the United States.

At Didcot there are engines and rolling stock of the Great Western Railway, a period signal box, a museum and a workshop where visitors can watch steam trains at work. But the high point is a ride in the comfort of the glorious days of railway travel. On these journeys into the past travellers can eat in spacious restaurant cars served by waitresses and proceed at a speed which, though regarded as fast at one time, today evokes the dignified calm of the days when gracious living was not just an empty phrase.

One of the most famous of the steam railways kept running by enthusiasts is the Bluebell Line, a 5-mile railway with a terminus at Sheffield Park, Sussex.

In addition to the sight of the splendid engines and the rides there is a great deal of interest for the practical-minded at Didcot where coaling, watering, repairs and maintenance are demonstrated as well as the highspeed pick-up and dropping of mail bags.

THROWING OFF WINTER'S TRACES

Traditionally, the equestrian event which opens the flat-racing season and is the harbinger of spring is the Lincolnshire Handicap, so-called because the race once took place at Lincoln. Today, however, the race takes place at the industrial city of Doncaster. Races have taken place at Doncaster since before 1615, so it is fitting that the first race (the Lincolnshire Handicap) and the last race (the St. Leger) of the season should be run here on the course at Town Moor, one of the oldest public moors in Britain.

The Lincoln is run over 1600 m (a straight mile), usually taking place at the end of March. It is a handicap race, which means that horses carry different weights according to their ability as assessed by the official handicapper. Because of its role in the opening of the season, the Lincolnshire Handicap attracts large crowds – and this lively scene is one that will be repeated at flat-racing courses throughout the summer.

The meeting is presided over by the Stewards of the course, appointed by the Jockey Club. Their duty is to ensure that all the rules of racing are

Opposite: Didcot in Berkshire is the home of the Didcot Railway Centre where steam engines of the Great Western Railway still hiss and clatter over an old line.

Below: The Doncaster racecourse in South Yorkshire is the setting for the first and last great races of the flat racing season, the Lincoln and the St. Leger.

In contrast to steeplechasing which is a professional sport nowadays run over fenced courses, a point-to-point is a cross-country competition between amateur riders of local hunts.

observed and to punish all infringements, including foul riding by the jockeys, who can be penalized for bumping, jostling or cutting across horses during a race. There are other racecourse officials with specific duties. The Clerk of the Course is responsible for the administration of the course and the condition of the track, the stands and the catering facilities. The Clerk of the Scales superintends the weighing-in before the race and the weighing-out afterwards. He is also in charge of the boards giving details of runners and riders and he draws lots for the starting positions. The job of lining up the runners at the starting post falls to the Starter and the Judge records the placing of the first six horses across the finishing line and also estimates the distances between them.

The excitement of Doncaster and all the other race meetings that follow it lies, for most people, in the atmosphere of a racecourse. Crowds mill about, pressing round the parade ring where the handsome thoroughbreds can be seen ridden by the jockeys brightly clad in the owners' colours. The colourful bookies signal to each other in a private semaphore which will establish the odds on the horses; people queue up at the totalizator as the computer works out the mathematical odds on each horse, based on the amount of money placed. As the Starter opens the starting gate a shout rises from the crowds pressed against the rails or sitting in the stands. 'They're off!' Necks crane forward, fingers tighten on racing programmes and the flat-racing season is under way.

For the punter, the Lincoln is traditionally linked with the Grand National at Aintree. A bet may be placed called The Spring Double, whereby a bet on a winner or placed horse at Doncaster is carried on to the Grand National. If the horse backed in the National is then placed as well, the punter can congratulate himself on an extremely lucrative and happy start to the season.

The Grand National is one of the great British sporting occasions. It has been the subject of country-wide concern in recent years, when the course, which has been in the hands of the Topham family for many years, was at risk. Sadly, the high quality television coverage of the race has tended to decrease the number of people who attend, and the subsequent loss of revenue has raised questions of the viability of holding the steeplechase at Aintree. At present, the meeting is sponsored by Ladbroke, but its ultimate fate remains in the balance.

A steeplechase was first organized on the Aintree course in 1839 by William Lynn, a local hotel keeper, who had leased the land from the 2nd Earl of Sefton. The terms under which Lynn was granted the right to run a race were that a sweepstake of 10 sovereigns each, with £100 added by the town of Liverpool, should take place. Also, horses of all types were to run, being handicapped according to age. The course was approximately the same as that of today, but it was not fenced and at the jumps the ground was not sloped as it is now. Originally named the Liverpool and National Steeplechase, it acquired the title of Grand National in 1847. The present course is over 7200 m (4 miles and 856 yds) and horses must make thirty jumps in all. Among them are such formidable obstacles as Becher's Brook, the Canal Turn and Valentine's – though sometimes they are not the cause of the worst accidents. The most memorable disaster of recent years took place in 1967 when practically all the competitors crashed at the twenty-third fence and the race was won by a fairly undistinguished horse called Foinavon which managed to avoid the melée.

Because of its testing nature the Aintree course is one over which chance plays an important part and there is never a sure winner. Few have won the race more than once, but there are outstanding exceptions: the remarkable steeplechaser, Red Rum, has won three times, ridden twice by Brian

The Chair is one of the narrowest jumps on the Grand National steeplechase at Aintree and often causes trouble for the competitors.

Racing at Cheltenham, where the countryside forms a lovely backdrop to the racecourse.

Fletcher and once by Tommy Stack. Among jockeys, the feat of G. Stevens, who won five times in the early years of the National, has never been repeated. However, his contemporary T. Oliver won four times, T. Beasley and A. Nightingall both notched up three wins in the closing years of the 19th century, and E. Piggott won three times between 1912 and 1919. These jockeys' performances have not been surpassed

Most riders dream of winning the National, but this is not the only reason for taking part. For some the race has an irresistible attraction. A notable example is the Duke of Albuquerque, a Spanish nobleman who first saw the Grand National on a film in the 1920s when he was a boy and was immediately bewitched by it. He rode his first National in 1952 and continued to ride in it, despite broken ribs and other injuries, until 1977, when the Jockey Club ruled it was time for a man of 57 to give up the dangerous sport. During his career as a National rider the Duke was placed seventh and eighth and had high hopes of winning in the year that he was obliged to retire! The same kind of tenacity and courage was demonstrated by Dick Francis, now a well-known thriller writer, who rode in the National eight times between 1949 and 1956. Early in his career he came in second to Russian Hero and was in the lead in 1956 on the Queen Mother's horse, Devon Loch, when it mysteriously collapsed a few yards from the finishing post.

Though the National is the most outstanding single event of the spring equestrian season, its star quality does not eclipse the other great meetings at Cheltenham and at Badminton.

The Cheltenham National Hunt meeting consists of several days' racing, climaxing in the Cheltenham Gold Cup. The course is beautifully situated just over a mile north-east of the town, on the western edge of the Cotswolds. The meeting provides the visitor with an opportunity not only to attend the most important steeplechase meeting in Britain, but also to enjoy one of its most elegant towns and some of its prettiest countryside. For these reasons the Cheltenham National Hunt is extremely well patronized and accommodation is hard to come by during National Hunt week.

The town itself came into prominence in the 18th century when Captain Henry Skillicorne, a retired privateer, discovered a medicinal spring and, putting his entrepreneurial skills to a new venture, built an Assembly Room on the site. As so often happens with pioneer business ventures, others quickly found their own springs; soon pump houses, venues for social assembly and housing to accommodate the visitors were springing up everywhere. Joseph Pitt, M.P. had the Pittville Pump Room erected, a place that still dispenses medicinal waters. The Rotunda was built in 1817 and the terrace of houses along the Promenade in 1823. Soon Cheltenham

The long oval paddock at the Cheltenham racecourse provides spectators with an opportunity to examine the thoroughbreds paraded in the ring before the races.

was competing in the spa business, which offered health, together with social gatherings, to the leisured classes of the day. Eventually its popularity waned, as the habit of taking holidays at health spas was replaced by the seaside holiday fashion. In recent years, however, Cheltenham has recovered much of its former popularity as a leisure centre. Taking the waters is no longer the main attraction – though many still do – the calendar of events and the charm of the town's architecture attract thousands of visitors. The town is also used as a base for explorations of the delightful Cotswold villages, the Roman villa at Chedworth and the Roman town of Cirencester.

The Cheltenham National Hunt is one of the first events of the spring calendar – though one of the last of the National Hunt season. It takes place in March and is one of the most important steeplechase meetings in Britain. The course, in accordance with National Hunt rules, is at least 2 miles long for each race and there are six birch fences 1.37 m (4 ft 6 ins) high and a ditch for every mile, plus at least one water jump. In the Gold Cup horses carry 76 kg (12 stone) each, unlike the Grand National where weights vary according to the handicap assessment, and the race is run over 5250 m (3 miles, 2 furlongs, 76 yards). Among the famous winners have been such horses as Golden Miller, who won no less than five years in succession, from 1932 to 1936; Cottage Rake who won three times, from 1948 to 1950 and Arkle, from 1964 to 1966. Arkle's statue stands by the Parade ring and his name is commemorated in the Arkle Challenge Cup Trophy, a race for novices. Other important races of the Cheltenham meeting are the Foxhunters Challenge Cup, the Cathcart Chase for hunt members or amateur jockeys, and the Grand Military Cup.

A very different kind of equestrian event in springtime is the Badminton Horse Trials, which take place in the lovely wooded parkland of the Duke of Beaufort's estate at Badminton. These Trials have an English country-life atmosphere that is without equal.

Below: At Minchinhampton, an attractive Cotswolds village, the old market building stands on the square facing the old market cross.

The three-day event at Badminton is one of the great equestrian meetings of the world. Here Captain Mark Phillips easily clears one of the jumps.

Though farther from the Trials than Cheltenham is from the National Hunt meeting, Bath is usually full at the time of the Badminton events, and it would be difficult to find a more delightful place to stay. Like Cheltenham, Bath owes its popularity to the warm springs that well up in its centre. The Romans first developed these and their splendid baths are still one of the many attractions of the cathedral city. The elegant Bath that one sees today belongs, however, to the 18th century, when John Wood and his son built the lovely Royal Crescent and the Assembly Rooms, and Robert Adam added the entrancing Pulteney Bridge with its little shops. Bath was then the centre of the English social scene, with Beau Nash laying down the law on morals and manners and everyone who was anyone – from Nelson to William Pitt, from Dr. Johnson to Jane Austen – staying or living there. Today the Hot Springs Physical Treatment Centre continues to provide health-giving waters and the city has a full calendar of entertainments and festivals.

Those who do not stay in Bath can take their pick of a wide selection of charming towns and villages, many built in the warm Cotswold stone which gives special character to their houses whether they be simple cottages or country manors. Bradford-on-Avon, to the east of Bath, is particularly noteworthy and has a fine old church with foundations dating back to the 8th century. To the north-east of Badminton lies the heart of the southern Cotswolds with Tetbury at its centre, and Malmesbury with its fine ruined Abbey to the east. To the west lies the old market town of Chipping Sodbury.

During the trials week most of the roads converging on Badminton are crowded with cars. The parking facilities, however, are good, and soon the occupants of the vehicles are walking over the tree-covered slopes of the Duke of Beaufort's estate. The traditional wear for a country event like Badminton is macs and wellingtons, with a preponderance of tweedy garments and ladies wearing colourful headscarves – all making up a typically English scene.

The Badminton Horse Trials were the happy inspiration of the 10th Duke of Beaufort, who was so downcast by the performance of the British team in the 1948 Olympic Games in London that he decided to allow his estate to be used for horse trials which would be open to all national riders. Until then, the events which are a feature of the Badminton Trials had been almost exclusively a military exercise and riders at the Olympic Trials were largely recruited from the Cavalry. The Duke's initiative introduced a new concept of trials and soon civilian riders were improving the standard of British performance and carrying off one of the world's most coveted prizes.

The Badminton Horse Trials exhibit three aspects of horsemanship: dressage, cross-country endurance tests and show jumping. The first day of the trials is devoted to a study of the grounds and examination of the competing horses by veterinary surgeons. The dressage takes place over two days. Dressage is the French term for the training of horses, and the competitors are judged on the balance between a horse's physique and its performance of manoeuvres in response to the rider's signals. High achievement in this discipline depends upon a great deal of cooperation and understanding between horse and rider, and the more effortless this appears the higher the marks a horse and rider are likely to achieve.

The cross-country is the high point of the Badminton meeting and takes place on the third day of the trials. It starts with a road and track section of about 6 miles, followed by a steeplechase of about 2 miles and then another road and track section. Finally comes the most testing part of the course as the horses and riders set off at intervals along a cross-country course of some 4–5 miles, riding across open country and through woods, jumping a series of testing obstacles, including a water jump, drop jumps, logs and hurdles along the way. Spectators can watch from almost any part of the course and can move about during the day to watch the performances of horses and riders over the various distances.

The freedom of movement over the park-like countryside (mounted stewards blow warning whistles when competitors are approaching) and the glorious spectacle of fine horses and riders, together with the beauty of the English countryside in springtime, makes Badminton one of the most glorious events of the British year. It is an event which gathers together Royalty, the aristocracy, celebrities and ordinary people in an apotheosis of the British love of equestrian sports. Since Badminton began, British performance in three-day eventing has gained world-wide prestige, with British riders such as Lucinda Green (née Prior Palmer), Mark Phillips and Richard Meade bringing home prizes from abroad and from the Olympics.

Newmarket in Cambridgeshire is on the edge of the flat fenlands that stretch from Cambridge to the Wash and the East Anglian coast, and is another gathering place for racing enthusiasts. The reason is that two of the great classics of flat racing take place here – the One Thousand and Two Thousand Guineas. The course has been a racing centre since the time of Charles II and its mile stretch is called the Rowley Mile after the King's favourite horse. It was here that the Jockey Club was formed in 1750, an event that promoted the expansion of horse-racing among a wider public. The Club's headquarters are still in the town. The racecourse and National Stud lie to the south-west of Newmarket. Nearby is the old Rutland Arms pub, which dates back to before the time of

Charles II, a place where flat race enthusiasts have gathered for over 400 years. The first of the two classic races to be established was the Two Thousand Guineas, which is run over the Rowley Mile and is a test of speed for the best thoroughbreds in Britain. This race was first run in 1809 and a few years later, in 1814, was followed by the One Thousand Guineas.

Cambridge, stretching along the River Cam, lies 13 miles from Newmarket and after the melée and excitement of the racecourse a stroll through the grounds and courtyards of the Cambridge colleges makes a soothing contrast. King's, with its glorious chapel, is entered from the busy high street, the King's Parade, and nearby are Clare and Queen's with their smooth riverside lawns. To the east of King's Parade are Corpus Christi, Pembroke and the Fitzwilliam Museum in Trumpington Street; and to the west, Trinity College, which possesses a Wren library. Along the northern stretch of the Cam is the Bridge of Sighs, so called because of its similarity to the bridge linking the Doge's Palace with the dungeons in Venice through which prisoners were led to trial or execution. This bridge joins St. John's College to the west bank, on which is situated Magdalene College and its Pepysian Library.

The surrounding Cambridgeshire countryside contains many villages which embody the spirit of rural England. Small hotels and inns provide attractive accommodation not only for racegoers, but also for the many visitors touring this historic region of England. Grantchester is probably

Opposite: The Mathematical bridge at Cambridge spans the River Cam at Queen's College. It was designed by William Etheridge in 1749 solely in wood but when dismantled and re-assembled in the 19th century metal was used to keep it together.

Below: Belvoir Castle in Leicestershire, home of the Duke and Duchess of Rutland, is the scene of many stirring events. The present castle was rebuilt in the 19th century.

the best known of the nearby villages, having been made famous by the poetry of Rupert Brooke. Some 15 miles to the north-west, along the River Ouse, are lovely villages with thatched, half-timbered houses, such as at St. Ives, Hemingford Abbots and Hemingford Grey.

Farther north-west the land rises away from the fens into the hills of the Midlands – a country of rich farmland where much of the medieval history of England was made. Powerful lords and barons erected castles here, which were to become stately manor houses once law and order was established under a unified monarchy. An echo of the feudal period remains at Belvoir Castle, near Grantham in Lincolnshire, home of the Duke and Duchess of Rutland, when jousting tournaments take place during the spring and summer.

The first Belvoir Castle was built in the 11th century by Robert de Todeni, who had arrived from Normandy with William the Conqueror. The castle fell into disuse and, in the 16th century, was presented to the Manners family, ancestors of the present owners. After a fire in 1814 it was rebuilt by the architect James Wyatt and was enlarged and refurbished in the 19th century by, among others, Matthew Wyatt (descendant of James) who designed the Elizabethan Salon in the style of Louis XIV. As well as this splendid room, the castle has other features of interest including a 17th and 21st Lancers Museum and a superb collection of paintings by artists such as Poussin, Holbein, Rubens and Reynolds in addition to many objects d'art and tapestries.

The medieval jousting tournaments take place in front of the castle terraces from which spectators view the lively scene of knights and horses dressed in the colours of their various manors. The tournament is conducted according to the rules laid down by Richard the Lionheart, who overcame the prejudices of the Church about what was then a highly dangerous military sport. Richard defined the sport of knights as jousting or tournaments; the former being an encounter between single knights and the latter a mock battle between teams of mounted men. The jousts were of two kinds: those à plaisance were basically friendly encounters and those à l'outrance took place to settle a disagreement between knights and were fought until one or other was maimed or killed. During and after the reign of Richard, royal permission was required for the holding of jousts or tournaments.

The underlying motive for jousts and tournaments was their usefulness in keeping knights in training for service either in regional warfare or in the hundred years of warfare carried on between England and France during the 14th and 15th centuries. The tournaments were also great social occasions attended by kings, lords and their courts, as well as the partisan crowds who were there to cheer and gamble on the success of their favoured knights. Ladies attended the tournaments and it became a custom for each knight to dedicate a victory to the lady of his choice. Often the ladies gave a token, perhaps a handkerchief or flower, which the knight fixed to himself or his horse – a custom which, in our less subtle times, has resulted in ladies presenting bras or tights to their favoured knights!

The jousting tournament at Belvoir begins with a parade and a series of tilts at the quintain. The quintain is a weighted sack on a swivelled arm which, if not struck correctly by the knight's lance, sweeps round behind him and hits him in the back, often unhorsing him. After this practice run, the knights begin their tilts, riding at each other along a separating fence and attempting to strike the other's shield or, best of all, to unhorse their rival. If the tilt is indecisive or if one of the knights feels dissatisfied with the result, there follows a joust à l'outrance with the knights continuing to fight (on foot, if they have been unhorsed) until one loses his helmet or falls to the ground and surrenders. After the individual jousts comes the

Left: Two colourful medieval knights engage in mock mortal combat at a jousting tournament at Belvoir Castle.

tournament, with the two groups of knights fighting in a *grande melée* in which all weapons are permitted including maces, axes and a fearsome star-shaped piece of metal attached to a pole by a chain.

Today, jousting is simply for fun but even in the early days it is doubtful if many knights were either killed or seriously wounded, though Henry II of France was killed in a joust. Knights were too valuable an asset to an ambitious king or lord and were better saved to fight another day than to be destroyed in a tournament.

Jousting tournaments at Belvoir take place several times during the spring and summer; other events such as veteran car rallies, cycle rallies and falconry are held during intervening weekends.

A quite different kind of spring equestrian event, also held in the grounds of an ancient castle, is the Royal Windsor Horse Show. This five-day show takes place in the Home Park, situated between Windsor Castle and Old Windsor, which is set along the Thames. The Windsor Horse

Above: Windsor Castle seen from Eton. The college chapel is on the left and the castle's round tower, built by Henry II and heightened by George IV, dominates the skyline in the centre of the picture.

The Household Cavalry give the Royal Windsor Horse Show a touch of glamour as they perform their musical ride.

Show originated in 1943 as a fund-raiser for the Wings of Victory campaign and has grown in importance every year. Not only does it provide a colourful and varied spectacle, but it is also a royal occasion, well supported by the Royal Family, who participate in the jumping and coach driving events, with some successes for Prince Philip and the Prince of Wales.

The events of the show take place in various rings and over a cross-country course. There is a central area with marquees offering refreshments and shops selling all kinds of equestrian gear as well as country crafts. There are stands from which the show jumping can be watched. One of the high spots of the spectacle is the musical ride by the Household Cavalry and another is the massed band display by the Guards. In addition, there are meetings of hounds and some children's events. The main business of the show is the jumping, however, and an event called the coach marathon which consists of three sections; the dressage, the marathon and the obstacle drive – providing plenty of thrills for both drivers and spectators.

The setting of the show is unique, with Windsor Castle nearby and the whole town of Windsor in festive mood. The Castle, originally a hunting lodge for William the Conqueror, is a great attraction for visitors. The ancient walled building, which first became a royal residence in the time of Henry I, incorporates the architecture of many eras of British history, including that of the Plantagenets, the Tudors, the Stuarts and the present House of Windsor. The Castle is divided into three sections: the Upper, Middle and Lower Wards, each with special features of interest. In the Upper Ward are the State Apartments which date from the time of Edward III, the Middle Ward is dominated by the massive Round Tower from the reign of Henry II and in the Lower Ward is the superb St. George's Chapel, built by Edward IV and Henry VIII. It is in the chapel that the religious ceremony following the Investiture of Knights of the Garter takes place.

Victorian England is commemorated in a charming and evocative manner just outside the castle at the railway station. This has been converted into a large-scale waxwork tableaux depicting the arrival of Queen Victoria at Windsor. She is shown alighting at the platform where she is received by celebrities of the period, and she also appears in the station forecourt, where a guard of honour salutes her with military precision.

Another evocation of the past is to be found in the cobbled streets around the Guildhall, built by Sir Christopher Wren in 1689, which stands on the busy High Street where there are well maintained shops and restaurants to cater for visitors. To the south of the town, and running alongside Home Park, is Windsor Great Park – a lovely parkland, typical of the best of southern English countryside. With its woods, streams and ponds, and a fine arboretum and gardens, it is a wonderful place to enjoy a picnic during the Royal Windsor Horse Show.

Also for those with an interest in the countryside is the Royal Ulster Agricultural Show, held at Balmoral 3 miles to the south of Belfast. This is

The 17th-century Guildhall in Windsor's High Street was completed by Sir Christopher Wren and is now a museum which houses the town's historical records.

the showplace of Northern Ireland farming and has been in existence since 1854, although it was originally held in the city itself. The present permanent showground of 14.2 hectares (35 acres) was first used in 1896 and since then has been the site of one of the major agricultural shows in Britain. Today, the show is much expanded and provides not only a gathering place for the farming community but also for urban dwellers attracted to the show for its sports and entertainments.

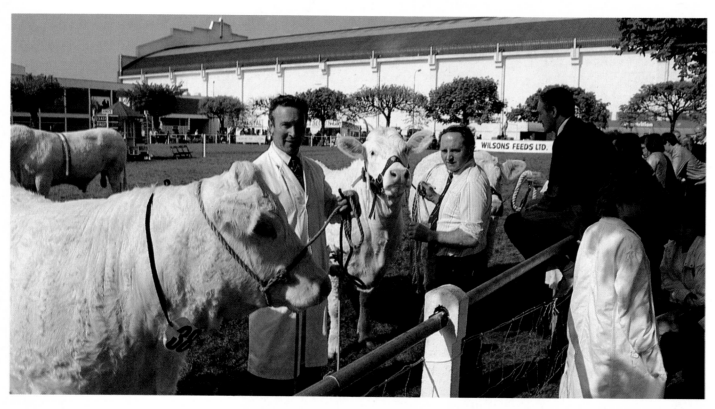

The Royal Ulster Agricultural Show, which takes place at Balmoral near Belfast, is noted for its fine cattle seen here under the sharp eyes of expert judges.

The centres of activity in the showground are the main ring and the two horse rings, where events and judging of livestock take place. Among the traditional popular events are the show jumping, an event with a particular attraction for the Irish, and fox hound demonstrations. There is also an event which is unusual in Britain, sheep shearing, and a special day for children's events.

Of a less country character are such events as the motorbike competitions and the flight of hot air balloons, whose bright colours make an impressive spectacle as they rise over the showground.

EPIC STRUGGLES

The struggle between groups of young men for the possession of barrels of beer or pieces of hare pie were once regular features of spring celebrations. They were usually unruly affairs in which anyone with blood coursing through his veins could take part and which caused consternation, and sometimes injury, to player and onlooker alike. It was inevitable, therefore, in the course of time and with the increase in population after the 15th century, that these boisterous explosions of spring fever should be regulated and that rules of conduct and play should be laid down. This led to the organized game systems we know today. Though the exuberance was curbed, the enthusiasm for physical activity was not checked and, in fact, has grown in the centuries during which control has been exercised. Today, sport plays a very large part in British national life.

One of the earliest events in the sporting calendar is the Oxford v. Cambridge University Boat Race. This annual rowing competition on the River Thames has achieved an almost legendary stature. Each year it attracts not only the supporters from the rival universities but also visitors from all over Britain – and, indeed, the world – who line the banks and wear the partisan rosettes of pale blue (Cambridge) or dark blue (Oxford), indicating which crew they support.

There is no let-up in the gruelling Boat Race as the two university crews strive to take advantage of wind and currents over the 4½-mile course from Putney to Mortlake. Here Cambridge leads in the 1986 race.

Crowds line the banks of the Thames at Putney, starting point of the Boat Race between the Universities of Oxford and Cambridge.

The first race was held in 1829 at Henley-on-Thames, now the scene of Henley Royal Regatta. According to tradition, the choice of position at the starting line is dictated by the toss of a golden sovereign of that year. The present course was adopted in 1845 and runs from Putney to Mortlake on an acute northern bend of the river, with the Middlesex bank to the north and the Surrey bank to the south. The distance, described as 'Four and a Quarter Miles', is actually 4 miles 374 yards if crews maintain their theoretical best courses.

The race begins at Putney Bridge which crosses the Thames to the west of Chelsea and Fulham, areas that were largely open countryside when the first race was rowed. South of the river there are still green spaces to be found at Wimbledon Common and at Richmond Park, where the herds of deer are a reminder that this was once a royal hunting ground. The two eights, which in recent years have permitted lady coxwains (Oxford had one in 1981, and Cambridge in 1985), row north at the start of the race past the Fulham football ground, straining to arrive first at the bend of the river where an advantage can be gained by getting into the tidal stream that sweeps round the Surrey bank. As the crews approach the northern reach of the horseshoe bend the splendidly ornate, Victorian Hammersmith Bridge comes into view. On the right there is a terrace of mid-Georgian houses and to the left the grounds of St. Paul's School.

The crews shoot through the bridge and turn along the top of the loop, past Chiswick on the Middlesex bank, where the Palladian Chiswick House and Hogarth's humbler abode lie by the Great West Road leading out of London. Racing south along the eastern arm of the horseshoe, the crews glide under Barnes Bridge and past another terrace of attractive old houses, lined with cheering spectators.

The end is now in sight, and, even if one crew is several lengths ahead,

the efforts of each are undiminished. Accidents can happen at this stage – in 1978 the Cambridge boat filled up with water and sank in particularly disastrous weather conditions.

The finishing line lies at Mortlake, past Dukes Meadows and the Mortlake breweries. The thickest crowds are found here, along the towpath and the Mortlake Terrace. Cheers and applause greet the exhausted victors and losers before the crowd disperses to celebrate another Boat Race Day at the restaurants and pubs of Richmond and Kew.

Another team event which is arousing an increasing amount of interest both in Britain and abroad is the Rugby Championship that takes place between England, France, Ireland, Scotland and Wales. The contest is played throughout each winter, coming to a climax in spring when the fate of the teams in the Championship often hangs on the final matches. The Rugby Championship has been taking place since 1910, when the first International took place at Twickenham, across the river from the Royal Borough of Richmond.

Twickenham, though only one of the many grounds on which the Championship is played, is nevertheless regarded as the headquarters of rugby, and it is the ambition of teams from all rugby-playing countries to play there. This green rectangle used to be known as Billy Williams' cabbage patch, after the cricketer and rugby player whose enthusiasm brought about the purchase of the land. The first International here was between England and Wales, an encounter which still generates the maximum excitement. The Twickenham matches are as much a show as a game. Pre-match excitement is aided by bands and drum majorettes, while spectators, usually well wrapped up against the crisp early spring air, surreptitiously (for strong liquor is forbidden on the grounds) drink out of pocket flasks.

Bright scarves and hats in team colours are worn by spectators at the Rugby Union Cup Final in England's most hallowed rugby ground at Twickenham.

When the show is over the match begins. According to legend, rugby was first invented inadvertently at Rugby School. A boy named William Webb Ellis picked up the ball during a football game and carried it over the goal line one day in 1823. This story, though recorded on a plaque at Rugby School, is probably more fiction than fact; no one really knows how the game came into being. The first 'official' rules of rugby were laid down in 1846 and stated, among other things, that matches were to be declared drawn after five days or after three days if no goal had been scored! Like most early encounters in which a ball was kicked about, there was no limit to the number of players, and often there were more than 300 players taking part in one match. Eventually, however, the number of players per team was limited to 15, as was recorded at the Oxford and Cambridge match of 1875.

Broadly speaking, the game then developed along the lines which it follows today. A group of forwards (usually eight in number) act as the assault force who try to gain possession of the ball. The ball is then taken by the scrum half who passes it to his fly half. The fly half then feeds it out to the three-quarters, who execute those exciting and ingenious runs which are the high spot of any game. One player stays in the back position and acts as the last line of defence in the event of a breakaway by the three-quarters of the opposing team.

Though traditionally watched from open stands in considerable discomfort, rugby at Twickenham, like other sports, has developed a commercial aspect; companies provide lunch, seat tickets and, for those who do not want to brave the cold weather, television. Traditionalists view this trend with dismay, maintaining that anyone with a real interest in this particularly British sport should be prepared to face the rigours of spectating without being molly-coddled! Be that as it may, rugby remains a

The great international matches of the rugby season take place in packed stadiums. Here England in white shirts are playing against France.

game with a growing number of enthusiasts throughout the world and the spectacle of a Twickenham encounter is hard to rival.

Rugby and football both descended from the same chaotic brawl of the early ball games recorded in England as long ago as the 12th century. These ancient games were described by a writer of the early days as causing fighting, contentions, quarrel picking and even murder. In the 19th century the two forms of the game were established and rugby and football parted company. After the Second World War, as a result of the social revolution in leisure coupled with the arrival of television, football became not only Britain's but also the world's most popular sport. In the 1950s, investment in the sport increased as crowds of tens of thousands packed into stadiums, and football players soon took on the glamour of Hollywood filmstars.

Wembley was the site of the British Empire Exhibition of 1924 and its football pitch was opened a year earlier in order that the Cup Final should be played there. Since then it has been the regular venue of the final match between football clubs in the annual knock-out competition.

Cup Final day is the scene of frenzied activity as the supporters of the competing teams pour into London carrying banners and wearing hats, scarves and shirts proclaiming their team allegiance. To Londoners it seems that their city is under siege, and the authorities have to take precautions, such as the boarding up of the statue of Eros in Piccadilly Circus, to avoid damage by high-spirited supporters. Tickets for the Cup are at a premium and are bought on the black market at many times their original price. The darker side of the Cup Final is, however, only one small aspect of this great celebration of the national sport of football. On the whole the crowds are boisterous but well behaved; the high spirits of the young are generally expressed only in shouting, singing, wearing

The old rivals Liverpool and Everton meet at Wembley, not for the first time, to dispute the title of best Merseyside team.

Wembley stadium, scene of the great Cup Finals, holds some 150,000 spectators. The rest of the millions of football fans watch the matches on television but often still dressed for the occasion.

outrageous clothes and having one drink too many – just as they always have been since the earliest celebrations of spring.

As the thousands of spectators take their places in Wembley Stadium, the atmosphere becomes charged with tension which the authorities attempt to relieve by various preliminary events. Bands play, cheer leaders wave flags and the crowd bursts into spontaneous chants of 'We are the champions!' The Cup Final is a high point of the sport, but it is also a conflict between the two teams which have overcome all the others on their way through the championship. It therefore possesses all the characteristics of occasions of physical confrontation. Challenge is there, and courage and stamina – and the will to win. The manner in which the encounter takes place is a reflection of British life and for that reason alone is an occasion not to be missed.

The most popular sporting event of the British spring is without doubt the London Marathon, which attracts some 28,000 participants and several thousand more spectators. The vast crowd of runners comes from all parts of Britain and the world, and represents an amazingly comprehensive cross-section of human society. There are septuagenarians and teenagers, Olympic athletes and people in wheel chairs, people in the latest 'designer' running gear and eccentrics in an unimaginable variety of fancy dresses, including pairs dressed as pantomime horses and groups masquerading as Viking ships. In fact the London Marathon is that rare phenomenon, a serious sporting event and a fun-run combined. Not all the organizers of the event approve of the wilder aspects of the Marathon, but there is little they can do about it; the London Marathon has acquired a unique character of its own and is the most spectacular event of the marathon year.

The London Marathon began its popular career in 1981, when Olympic athletes Chris Brasher and John Disley designed the run. The start of the London Marathon at Blackheath is a popular gathering with thousands of spectators crowding the green lawns of the heath that lies above Greenwich near the Royal Observatory. From here the runners set off along a dual course towards the east, which allows time and distance for some space to develop between the runners before they come together again as they approach Woolwich. From Woolwich the runners head back west towards Greenwich along the lower road that runs parallel to the Thames. They enter Greenwich by the road between the National Maritime Museum, which includes the Queen's House, a former home of Henrietta Maria, the wife of Charles I, and the Greenwich Hospital, which was built by Wren and Hawksmoor on the site of Henry VIII's palace.

Yogi Bear may not have won the London Marathon but along with other light-hearted runners he added to the fun of the great race.

*The London Marathon runners are
still in close formation in the early
stages of the race as they pass the
magnificent* Cutty Sark, *last of the
tea clippers.*

Passing the *Cutty Sark*, with its tall elegant masts, and the smaller *Gipsy Moth IV*, in which Sir Francis Chichester sailed round the world, the runners now head for Tower Bridge. Once across the Thames they turn east once more into what was once the Port of London area, but is now a fast developing extension of the City. At the Isle of Dogs, described by residents at the time of writing as the world's largest building site, the runners turn west again for St. Katharine's Dock, a former commercial dock which now has pubs and shops and is used as a floating museum for interesting old ships and tugs. Passing under Tower Bridge the runners traverse the Thameside terraces between the Tower and Traitors' Gate and continue along Lower Thames Street where the Billingsgate fish market once operated and where remains of a Roman port have been discovered. On the way they pass St. Magnus the Martyr, a handsome Wren church crushed between characterless commercial buildings.

The route now runs parallel to the Thames with St. Paul's to its right and it then joins the Victoria Embankment after Blackfriars Bridge. The

The final tape of the London Marathon lies at the southern end of Westminster Bridge under a banner whose clock ticks away the time for each of the finishing contestants.

runners are now strung out as they jog along under the plane trees and past the moored ships of the Royal Naval Reserve and the Honourable Company of Master Mariners. Cleopatra's Needle rises above the Embankment here, a familiar sight to French and United States runners who know the companion obelisks in the Place de la Concorde in Paris and in Central Park, New York.

Beyond the Hungerford footbridge which crosses the Thames to the South Bank cultural complex, which can be seen clearly on the far side, the runners turn right up Northumberland Avenue to Trafalgar Square, where Nelson watches the Marathon wheel left under Admiralty Arch and disappear up the Mall. Buckingham Palace lies at the far end of the treelined avenue and there the runners turn left at Birdcage Walk and head for Parliament Square and the Houses of Parliament. An anxious look at the tower of Big Ben will tell the leaders whether they have made good time, but less well trained runners will look up at the familiar clock face with a sigh of relief. At the other end of Westminster Bridge is the finishing

This thatched cottage at Shottery near Stratford-upon-Avon preserves the tranquil atmosphere of the times when William Shakespeare courted Ann Hathaway at her home.

line and the elation that comes to those who have achieved their targets.

Despite its informal and fun-run character, the Marathon has a surprising number (over 90 per cent) who complete the course, spurred on perhaps by a will to meet the challenge of a long gruelling run or because they are earning money for charity by doing so. There is also the exhilaration of having taken part in a run which passes many of London's most historic places and of having jogged through history from the time of the Romans to the present day.

THE GENTLE SIDE OF SPRING
There are gentler springtime occasions which can give rewarding glimpses of life in Britain. Among these are the traditional and artistic events which take place in spring and then run on into the summer.

A British April festival which has a worldwide significance is the one that commemorates Shakespeare's birthday, for the great Elizabethan dramatist has crossed all frontiers and speaks to all the world in the diversity of its languages. William Shakespeare was born in Stratford-upon-Avon in April 1564, and probably lived there with his parents and his two brothers and four sisters until he went to London around 1585. The house he was born in with its timbered front and red tiled roof has been carefully preserved and is a memorial to the great playwright.

He was evidently a bright pupil at the school he attended, which still retains the appearance that it had in Elizabethan times, with its beamed ceiling and timber and plaster walls. And it was probably there that he first came across the classical authors that would open the gates of literature to him. Almost immediately after leaving school he married Ann

Hathaway, some eight years older than he and the daughter of a well-off yeoman family. A daughter, Susanna, and twins Hamnet and Judith, were born in the next three years and soon after Shakespeare left for London.

Shakespeare's birthday is commemorated in a four-day festival which begins with a military march through the town accompanied by bands, which give an appropriate touch of pageantry to a festival celebrating the author of such stirring historical dramas.

The second day of the festival acknowledges the world-wide interest in the famous playwright by a morning reception in the Shakespeare Memorial Theatre for ambassadors, representatives of overseas dominions and other distinguished guests. There are then various entertainments which include dancing displays and band concerts as well as a floral procession to Shakespeare's tomb in the parish church of the Holy Trinity, which is surrounded by a pretty churchyard and overlooks the River Avon.

During the commemorative weekend Stratford receives a host of visitors and there are special exhibitions and events at all the places connected with the playwright, including recitals, concerts and folk dancing. The Shakespeare centre puts on a special exhibition. On the Saturday evening there is a special performance at the Shakespeare Memorial Theatre and on the Sunday a Shakespeare service in Holy Trinity Church.

The occasion is a quiet one on the whole, providing an opportunity to pay tribute to the greatest poet and playwright of all time. His early home, his school, the house of his daughter, Susanna, and the gardens of the house which he bought after he achieved success in London are all evocative of his life and the period in which he lived, as is Ann Hathaway's home at nearby Shottery.

London's Chelsea was a favourite haunt of Charles II, who built the Royal Hospital for wounded soldiers, prompted, it is said, by his mistress

Above: The serene north facade of the Royal Hospital in Chelsea designed by Sir Christopher Wren between 1682 and 1692. The elegant building has been a home for old and disabled soldiers since its foundation.

Opposite: A procession of distinguished visitors from all over the world parade through Stratford-upon-Avon to pay tribute to the world's greatest dramatist.

Nell Gwynne. This splendid building, still inhabited by old soldiers who are seen on festive days in their proud red coats and tricorn hats, has 9.3 hectares (23 acres) of gardens in which the Flower Show of the Royal Horticultural Society takes place. The grounds, which lie to the west of Chelsea Bridge and stretch down to the Embankment, overlook the River Thames and, on the south bank, Battersea Park. Originally these were the Ranelagh Gardens – a Chelsea pleasure park. Chelsea had become popular in Tudor times: Sir Thomas More lived there at Beaufort House, Henry VIII built a manor house there and Elizabeth I lived in the area for some years. In the 19th century the quarter became the favourite residence for artists, among whom Turner and Whistler are best remembered, and writers such as Thomas Carlyle (whose house is now a museum), Oscar Wilde and the American, Mark Twain, made it their home.

The Royal Horticultural Society, established in 1804 at Hatchards Bookshop in Piccadilly, was founded for the improvement of horticulture at a time when Britain's exploration of the world was adding countless new and exotic plants to British gardens. Among the founders were Sir Joseph Banks, a botanist who had sailed around the world with Captain James Cook and John Wedgwood, son of the famous pottery manufacturer. Throughout the 19th century the Society held its shows first in Chiswick and later at the Inner Temple, off Fleet Street in the City of London. In 1911 it moved to the grounds of the Chelsea Hospital and the following year the show was opened by George V. Since then the Chelsea Flower Show has been not only a gathering of professional nurserymen, landscape and market gardeners, but also a brilliant social occasion which the Queen always visits the day before the official opening.

The centre of the show is the huge 1.3-hectare ($3\frac{1}{4}$-acre) marquee in which flowers grown especially for the occasion are exhibited. Many of

Above: The glory of summer gets a preview at the Chelsea Flower Show in May when gardeners from all over Britain, and some from overseas, show off the products of their skills.

Opposite: The Royal Hospital was founded by Charles II at the instigation of Sir Stephen Fox, and not Nell Gwynne as romantic legend insists. On Founders Day the Chelsea Pensioners look their best in their bright red coats and tricorn hats.

Preceding page: Street theatre is one of the attractions of Brighton's International Festival which attracts both amateur talent and professional artists from many countries.

these are grown out of season and others have arrived from distant destinations, sponsored by the governments of countries all over the globe. The show does not confine itself to flowers, however, and there are vegetables, herbs, rockplants and shrubs competing for Gold Medals in their own categories.

Inevitably, the marquee gets extremely crowded with a vast number of visitors during the four days of the show. People from a complete cross-section of British society attend the show, for gardening is a national

hobby. Many visitors take picnics to the show and can be seen enjoying their lunch on the green lawns if the weather is kind, as it often is during the British spring.

One of the largest English art festivals takes place in May at Brighton, the south coast resort which became the centre of fashionable life under the Prince of Wales, later George IV. Even before the Prince arrived and set up house with Mrs. Fitzherbert, Brighton had begun to prosper as a spa thanks to Dr. Richard Russell, who was able to persuade a gullible public

that sea water, either drunk with milk or port or bathed in, was good for the health. The Prince of Wales gave the place social cachet and commissioned the architect John Nash to extend the Pavilion, originally built by Henry Holland, into the exotic fantasy it is today. A symbol now, as it was then, of the resort's racy image and reputation for fashion and entertainment.

Brighton has several festivals and galas throughout the year, the most important of which is the International Festival. The town, with its fine front bordered by Georgian houses, is an ideal a venue for an artistic festival. The Theatre Royal is renowned for the quality of its productions and there is a permanent concert hall, the Dome, as well as many other places suitable for concerts and shows, including the Royal Pavilion. Brighton itself has an almost theatrical atmosphere, with the narrow lanes of the old centre contrasting with the grand facades of Georgian buildings and the fussy bow-fronted houses of the turn of the century. The piers, too, are a relic of bygone times.

The Brighton Festival celebrated its 21st birthday in 1987 with a programme based on northern European culture and the theme of Myth, Magic and Legend which underlies so much of the north European cultural tradition. Traditionally the festival begins with a gathering on the lawns of the Royal Pavilion and a procession through the town. In 1987 the theme of the gathering was May Day with all its pagan associations and the Pavilion lawns were colourful with human and supernatural beings of May Day legend. The Maypole, banned by Parliament in 1644 because of its pagan symbolism, was much in evidence and so were morris dancers and musicians who led the colourful procession through the old town, accompanied by street entertainers. Buskers, jugglers, sword swallowers, fire eaters and the like always play an important part in the Brighton Festival, which is as much a popular event as one in which theatre, opera and music of the highest standards play their part.

At the Theatre Royal there are important productions, often going on to a London run after the festival and there is also opera by famous overseas companies. The Dome has opera performances by the New Sussex Opera company, which often commissions for the occasion special works in which well-known professional singers, designers and conductors take part. Classical concerts and choral music are usually performed at the Victorian Byzantine church of St. Bartholomew, and there are solo recitals at the Royal Pavilion.

At the other end of the musical scale there is a jazz festival within the main festival, in which famous jazz players from home and abroad take part and there are also rock concerts. During the festival Brighton has a multiplicity of other entertainments, which include flower shows and horse shows. There is also a regatta which commemorates the fact that Charles II, the 'Merry Monarch', escaped from the clutches of Cromwell's men at Shoreham and so survived to be the King who brought back the pursuit of pleasure into English life.

One of the most spectacular events is the grand firework display, a splendid sight as the rockets and fiery cascades burst over the sea, and there is an ongoing round of pleasure at restaurants and wine bars where itinerant musicians entertain. With so much going on, the visitor should not forget such traditional Brighton amusements as a ride on Volck's electric train, one of the first in England, which runs along the shore to Black Rock and the new marina.

The Brighton Festival lasts about three weeks and during this time there are many opportunities for visits to some of the fine downland countryside where old villages still nestle quietly in the folds of the hills, and country houses and castles dominate superb views.

Opposite: Fireworks over the sea at Brighton are a brilliant feature of the festival and illuminate the three-mile seafront with its two piers.

Summer Is 'Icumen' In

Summer in Scotland brings out the heather and fills the glens with fresh greenery. At Pitlochry, home of a famous theatre festival, the River Tummel runs fiercely through a narrow gorge.

The characteristic call of the cuckoo echoing through a woodland glade traditionally sends the British scurrying to their desks to pen letters to *The Times*, announcing that the cuckoo has arrived and is heralding the approach of summer: 'Sumer is icumen in, lhude sing cuccu' wrote the anonymous poet. But Frederick Delius, dedicating one of his tone poems to the first cuckoo of spring, suggests that there is some confusion about the opening seasons of the year. The British spring and summer merge gracefully. Some years, owing to the vagaries of the weather, the tender green leaves on the trees and the spring flowers in the hedgerows are still with us in June, starting the summer with a beautiful freshness. Britain's summer solstice has a spring-like air and most British

people regard the month of June as the beginning, rather than the height, of summer.

The summer festivities start in June, beginning with three great events: the Derby, Trooping the Colour and glorious, fashionable Royal Ascot. Shows and festivals abound during this period – in the countryside, in the courtyards of ancient castles, in the Highlands where the Scottish clans wear their proud tartans, and in the cities. This is the time for military occasions, showing that what the forces have lost in numbers since the great days of Empire, they have gained in expertise. Summer is also the time for music, opera and art in country settings, with the beauty of nature enhancing that of the arts.

Open-air concerts are a popular feature of summer. At Kenwood in north London orchestras play in an attractive lakeside setting in the grounds of elegant Kenwood House.

Burlington House, Piccadilly, home of the 3rd Earl of Burlington, was converted for use by the Royal Academy of Arts in the late 19th century. Exhibitions are held there throughout the year, including the Summer Exhibition, now a national institution.

THE BEGINNING OF THE SEASON

A major event that signals the beginning of the London season is the opening of the Royal Academy Summer Exhibition at Burlington House, Piccadilly. The original Burlington House was built in 1665 at the time when the area south of St. James's Church (a fine building by Sir Christopher Wren) was being developed as a fashionable quarter by Henry Jermyn. Admirably situated between Buckingham Palace and St. James's Palace, Green Park and Trafalgar Square, the quarter became a centre for coffee houses and other fashionable, but less innocuous, places. There were clubs such as Whites and Boodles, where gentlemen could gamble, and establishments nearby where they could entertain lady friends. Among these clubs' members have been celebrated poets such as Lord Byron and famous artists like Joshua Reynolds, the first president of the Royal Academy. The Academy held its first Summer Exhibition in 1769, under the patronage of George III. The exhibition was not held at Burlington House until nearly a hundred years later, in 1868, when the original house had been extended to include the present entrance courtyard, which has a statue of the first president in its centre. The new Burlington House buildings are home to a number of distinguished societies: the British Academy, the Society of Antiquaries, the Royal Astronomical Society and the Chemical and Geological Societies. The Royal Academy of Art is also based here and has its exhibition rooms and school of art in the Old Burlington House.

Since its installation at Burlington House, the opening of the Royal Academy Summer Exhibition has been a fashionable rendezvous for the aristocratic, rich, talented or otherwise distinguished members of society. In Victorian times these included not only members of high society, but

also such colourful and scandalous figures as Lily Langtry and Oscar Wilde. Today the Summer Exhibition is as popular as ever, not only among artists, who send in thousands of entries of which only about 1500 can be shown, but also among the public, whose eagerness to attend the opening day has led to the establishment of three such occasions before the show. The Exhibition, which is open to the public, receives nearly half a million visitors during the summer.

Though once rather academic in character, the Summer Exhibition is now a colourful display of the most outstanding work being done in Britain at the present time. There are rooms full of the paintings of established Academicians – a collection of works in numerous styles from Impressionist onwards. There are works by the latest avant-garde. You will find beautifully crafted miniatures and small paintings, huge canvases and collages, sculptures and even architectural drawings. With its colour and variety, the Academy Summer Exhibition is an appropriate opening to the London summer season.

Probably the most popular race meeting of the year is the Derby, which takes place on Epsom Downs. The race first took place in 1780, and was organized by General John Burgoyne and his friend Edward Stanley, later the 12th Earl of Derby. Burgoyne (the unhappy victim of government hesitancy during the war against America, when he was defeated at Saratoga) and Stanley were both typical 18th-century gentlemen – men of action who fought hard and played hard. The decision to launch the race was taken at The Oaks, Burgoyne's country house, where gentlemen and celebrities of the day gathered to enjoy boisterous all-night gambling parties. Horse-racing was a fashionable form of gambling at the time, and Anthony St. Leger had recently created the race known as the St. Leger, run at Doncaster. Inspired by his example, Lord Derby and Burgoyne

The annual Summer Exhibition at Burlington House attracts a world-wide public and provokes animated discussions about the state of art today. All the exhibits are for sale.

The slope and turn of the Epsom course at Tattenham corner challenges the skill of the jockeys seen here taking part in the Derby.

organized a race for fillies in 1779 and named it The Oaks, after the house. Delighted at winning this race with his filly, Bridget, Lord Derby also created a race for three-year-old colts and fillies – the Derby.

The first Derby, in 1780, was won by Sir Charles Bunbury's horse Diomed, cheered to victory by the crowds who were to set the lively style for Derby Days to come. Besides the excitement of the racing, much eating and drinking was enjoyed, and there were other diversions like cock fighting, bear baiting and wrestling matches to watch. After the Napoleonic Wars, Derby Day was attended by increasing numbers of enthusiasts, and public interest in horse-racing was reflected in the newspapers, which began to report meetings. A sporting paper, *Bell's Life*, was born and the passion for horse-racing swept the country without distinctions of class.

People from all levels of society enjoy Derby Day, whether they attend the occasion or merely watch it on television, having laid their bets at the local betting shop. The first monarch to attend the event was, curiously enough, Queen Victoria, but she did not repeat the visit. Her son, Edward VII, was an assiduous participant in the Derby and his horses won the race three times: in 1896 with Persimmon, four years later with Diamond Jubilee, and again in 1909 with Minoru.

Frith's painting of the 1858 Derby brings out the atmosphere of Derby Day marvellously, capturing the holiday mood which surrounds it to this day. From early morning the roads to Epsom are crowded with cars and coaches; the trains arriving at Epsom station are packed. Everyone has set out determined to enjoy themselves and some have high hopes of backing a winner. People set about the business of eating and drinking and earnestly study the form. Bookies take up their positions by the rails and start semaphoring odds while, all over the course, stewards make their last

minute preparations and television camera crews practise their routines. Unlike Ascot, the Derby attracts a wide cross-section of the population – there are usually some eccentrics at the course, entertaining the crowds with their extravagant outfits or by dancing, breathing fire or swallowing swords. There is also a regular fairground.

The Derby course is shaped like a horseshoe and rises 45 m (150 ft) in the first 800 m ($\frac{1}{2}$ mile). It then descends to the famous Tattenham Corner, where the course forces the horses to bunch together and competition is fierce. The race is a test of courage and stamina and winning is one of the highest aspirations of jockeys, trainers and owners. Among the most successful jockeys is Lester Piggott, who stands out with nine wins to his credit.

When Lord Derby held his first race at Epsom the Downs were still in the midst of the countryside but, over the years, London has spread outwards and the M25 motorway has brought an avalanche of traffic to the edges of the racecourse. To the south, however, the Surrey countryside retains much of its original character, with neat fields boxed in by tall hedgerows. Small villages and country houses nestle along the edges of the North Downs which sweep from Dover to Winchester before curving back eastward along the coast. To the west of Epsom lies the great ridge of Downs between Guildford and Dorking. In this area the market towns of Leatherhead, Cobham, Ripley and East Horsley provide hotels and restaurants where Epsom racegoers can stay or enjoy meals in delightful Tudor or Queen Anne buildings. In the 18th century many rich and aristocratic people built country houses in this lush part of the south-east and there are still plenty of them to see for those who want to combine the excitement of the racing with a glimpse into the background of its founders. Epsom itself rose to fame through its medicinal springs, which

It seems as if the whole of Britain has turned up to Derby Day in cars, double-decker buses, vans and coaches, but there is room for everyone on the Downs on this popular national race day.

produced the universal panacea of the 19th century – Epsom Salts. Today the town still retains vestiges of its spa, though most of its buildings reflect its involvement with horses rather than health. Dorking is a fine historic place where Dickens stayed. The writer includes the town in Mr. Pickwick's adventures. Nearby is Burford Bridge where Nelson held his last meeting with Lady Hamilton, and Keats completed 'Endymion'. The downland scenery in this area is exceptional, with Box Hill rising smoothly and steeply above the River Mole; Leith Hill, to the south, is the highest point of south-east England and provides panoramic views across the Sussex Weald.

Near Dorking, to the north-west, is the splendid mansion of Polesden Lacey with its famous gardens; to the west lies charming, rural Abinger Hammer, once a village of blacksmiths as the figure on the village clock testifies. Further west is Guildford with its steep main street. The remains of a castle built by Henry II and the 17th-century Angel Hotel, an old coaching inn, can be seen here. There are several outstanding country houses around Guildford: Clandon Park with its Palladian mansion, Hatchland on the road from Leatherhead, Elizabethan Sutton Place and Tudor Loseley Hall are all within easy reach.

THE ROYAL SUMMER

Perhaps the most significant of the ceremonies that take place on the threshold of summer is the Trooping the Colour ceremony, which is performed on the monarch's official birthday.

The custom of parading the regimental colours has a long and interesting history. In the early days of organized warfare, armies were made up of mercenaries, fighting for the lords who paid for their services rather than for nations or causes. Therefore it was necessary to familiarize the troops with the design of their employer's emblem so that, in the heat and confusion of battle, the soldiers would know where to rally when called. It thus became the custom to 'Troop the Colour' before the

Opposite: From Box Hill on the North Downs near Dorking there is a fine view across the valley of the River Mole.

Below: Polesden Lacey, an early 19th-century mansion, is beautifully furnished and has extensive views over the Downs from its famous gardens.

assembled armies. Later, when the English kings waged the Hundred Years War against France, the concept of duty to king and country was born. The sense of nationality, of belonging to your country, was a new idea and it inspired a new attitude in the English. The citizen had a duty and loyalty to his own country above any other. Symbols served to focus attention and to make tangible this new commitment; one of these symbols was the national flag. In this way, the regimental colours became more than just the identifying colours of a troop of soldiers and began to stand for honour, loyalty, courage and all the other virtues a good citizen owed to his country. Defending the colours in battle became a matter of honour. Today, Trooping the Colour reaffirms this tradition, making the ceremony particularly emotive in character.

The association with the monarch's birthday began in 1755, when the ceremony was performed for George II in order to establish a commitment

Preceding page: The solid ranks of the Household Cavalry on their superb horses make an unforgettable sight as they return down the Mall after the Trooping the Colour ceremony.

by the army and the people to a Hanoverian monarch who could hardly speak their language. The date of the monarch's 'official' birthday was established during the reign of Edward VII for the convenience of all concerned.

The ceremony takes place in the large open space of the Horse Guards Parade, behind the Horse Guards building designed by William Kent and facing St. James's Park, one of London's most beautiful parks. Crowds fill the stands specially erected all round the square. From the upper tiers of the stands there is a splendid view of the parade ground and the buildings of Whitehall. On the north side is the New Admiralty building, built in the late 19th century, and Admiralty House. On the south side of Horse Guards Parade is Dover House, the Scottish Office and the old Treasury – another 18th-century William Kent building – behind which can be seen the towers of the Houses of Parliament and Westminster Abbey.

Left: One of the most magnificent events of the year is Trooping the Colour at Horse Guards Parade, Whitehall. This takes place on the Sovereign's official birthday in June.

On the sanded parade ground the red-jacketed Foot Guards form a long L-shape, with each double column of soldiers perfectly aligned; in the centre the massed bands wait for the signal to begin their display. Later they are joined by the mounted band of the Household Cavalry, whose splendid uniforms, with shining cuirasses and plumed helmets always bring forth applause from the expectant crowds.

Until 1986, the Queen trooped the colour on horseback, but her favourite horse, Burmese, was then retired, and she decided not to train a new horse for this difficult and responsible task. Now the Queen is driven up the Mall in an open carriage. She inspects the guards from the carriage and then alights to take the salute from a dais. But nothing else about this magnificent event has changed. The drive down the Mall, lined with Guardsmen in their brilliant uniforms of black bearskins and scarlet tunics, is timed so that the Queen arrives at Horse Guards Parade at precisely eleven o'clock. She is preceded by other carriages containing members of the Royal Family, who are escorted by the band of the Household Cavalry. The Queen takes the salute as the colour is trooped and the bands play. This stirring sight is one which never loses its popularity. Even its previews (when the ceremony is rehearsed) are fully booked. On these occasions the colour is saluted by the Major General commanding the Household Division and the Colonel of the Regiment of the Colour – the Prince of Wales for the Welsh Guards, the Duke of Edinburgh for the Grenadier Guards and the Duke of Kent for the Scots Guards.

The second great royal occasion to take place in June is the Investiture of new Knights of the Most Noble Order of the Garter, at Windsor. The Garter is the highest Order in the land and the oldest Order of Chivalry, dating back to the time of Edward III. According to legend, the Order was created when the King was dancing with a lady who had the embarrassing misfortune to lose her garter. Picking it off the floor, the King fastened it round his partner's leg while exclaiming to his guests: 'Honi soit qui mal y pense' (Shamed be he who thinks evil of it). Whether or not the courtiers present were harbouring evil thoughts is not recorded, but the saying remained as the motto of the Order. A more prosaic explanation is that Edward, who was a warlike king and often in conflict with the Scots and the French, wished to reward the knights who had helped him to victory at Neville's Cross, Crécy and Poitiers, and did so by awarding 24 of them the Order of the Garter. Although the decline of feudalism and the decreasing power of the barons meant that the monarch did not need to depend on an élite of loyal lords, the Order of the Garter continued to be bestowed on those who served their king and country well. The awarding of the Order is solely the prerogative of the monarch, who is also the Head of the Order.

An Investiture of the Order is carried out privately in the Throne Room at Windsor Castle, before a gathering of Officers and the Knight Companions of the Order, guarded by the Yeomen of the Guard in their colourful Tudor uniforms. The Queen, accompanied by members of the Royal Family, sits on the Throne and the Knights elect are summoned one by one to the room by the Garter King of Arms and Black Rod. The Knight elect, accompanied by two Knights of the Order who are his sponsors, receives the insignia of the Order. The garter is affixed to the left leg of male knights and to the left arm of ladies.

After a lunch attended by all the Knights comes the public part of the ceremony. This consists of a procession from St. George's Hall, in the Royal Apartments, to St. George's Chapel in the Lower Ward of the Castle. The procession is led by the Constable and Governor of Windsor Castle, followed by the Military Knights of Windsor in scarlet uniforms –

Opposite: The newly invested Knights of the Garter accompanied by their peers walk from the royal apartments in Windsor Castle where the Investiture has taken place to St. George's Chapel, led in this picture by the Military Knights of Windsor.

In St. George's Chapel each Knight of the Garter, the highest order in the land, has his own stall in the choir over which hangs his personal banner.

95

The Queen's arrival in an open landau is a high point at Royal Ascot which is one of the summer's most glorious and fashionable occasions.

heralds and pursuivants of the College of Arms. Then come the Knights, in their splendid apparel of a dark blue mantle with the Star of the Order on the left breast, a crimson velvet hood and black velvet hat. The Knights are followed by members of the Royal Family and, finally, the Queen and Prince Philip. This splendid and unique occasion is made more memorable by the presence of the Household Cavalry and two military bands. Those who watch the unfolding of this colourful and dignified royal ceremony no doubt congratulate themselves on having had the foresight to apply for admission at an early date.

The ceremony concludes with a private service at St. George's Chapel, where the beautiful gothic interior is hung with the banners of the Knights of the Garter above their private choir stalls.

The day of the Garter Procession is followed by one of the most festive of royal occasions – Royal Ascot. Ascot Week takes place on land owned by the monarch and was begun in 1711 by Queen Anne, who was a keen horsewoman, and who presented the Queen's Plate with a 100 guinea prize for the winner. Though the object of the four-day meeting is the horse-racing, there is no doubt that the distinguishing feature of Royal Ascot is its fashionable and elegant atmosphere. This is best observed in the Royal Enclosure, where the ladies appear in finery designed by leading couturiers. A particular feature of the fashion show is the variety of splendid and outrageous hats vying for attention. The gentlemen of Ascot, however, play their role with traditional discretion, dressed in top hats and morning-suits.

The glamorous social aspects of Ascot grew as royalty gave it more and more support. Though Queen Anne had established the course, it was not until the time of George IV, the 'bon viveur king', that a royal procession preceded the racing and the day became a champagne and lobster

occasion. Edward VII carried royal participation even further, arranging for his chef to supply magnificent lunches in the Royal Box. He also raced his own horses, several of which were successful – much to the delight of the crowds who always cheered lustily when the popular King drove up the course in his landau. Today the gourmet aspects of a royal presence are less in evidence but not the enthusiasm for royal entries in the races. Queen Elizabeth II breeds and races her own horses and, when she arrives in her landau for the pre-meeting drive up the course, there are cheers from the crowds and shouts of 'Good luck, Ma'am' as she arrives at the Grand Stand and the world's most elegant race meeting gets under way.

The Ascot racecourse is beautifully situated to the south-west of Windsor Great Park and consists of a triangular course of 4000 m (2½ miles). The course is flat, with an easy curve which allows horses to gallop freely. The most important races on the card are the Queen Anne Stakes, the Hardwicke Stakes, the Kings Stand Stakes (for sprinters), the King Edward VII Stakes, the Queen Mary Stakes (for two-year-old fillies), the Coronation Stakes and the Gold Cup.

Ascot and Windsor stand at the very western edge of the London sprawl and beyond lie stretches of countryside which are eyed enviously by developers, but are fiercely guarded by those who want to preserve this lovely and historic part of England. From here to Oxford the Thames Valley is full of ancient villages and riverside towns which retain much of the atmosphere of the Victorian and Edwardian Ages when the river had become a great pleasure ground. Steamers and rowing boats provided a day on the water for families, and young men took their lady-friends out for an afternoon's punting at Maidenhead. The river was also the venue for the sportsmen who vied with each other, either singly or in teams, for rowing honours. At Henley-on-Thames, two weeks after the racing at

Grey 'toppers' predominate in this picture of Royal Ascot but the race meeting is also renowned for the originality of ladies' hats.

The Ascot race track with its easy turns and absence of gradients makes for fast finishes which provide plenty of excitement for the vast crowds.

Ascot, fashionable society would don its regatta gear. Women in white muslin dresses and straw hats and men in white ducks and blazers would watch the races either from the banks or from rowing boats moored at the finishing post. The occasion began under the patronage of Prince Albert in 1851 and has continued, relatively unchanged, until the present day.

It would be difficult to find a lovelier situation for the Royal Regatta than Henley, a town on the north bank of the Thames, nestling between the wooded slopes of the Chiltern Hills. Along the river bank is a terrace of old boathouses, now used as an art gallery, and a pub. The red brick hotel, the Red Lion, was once a coaching inn, and has provided shelter for such eminent figures as Charles I, George II and Boswell. The fine 18th-century stone bridge spans the river at this point and to the north of the bridge is the High Street, with its Town Hall surrounded by elegant Georgian houses. To the south of the bridge is the famous Leander Club, centre of activities during the Regatta. Striped canvas boathouses and marquees line the river bank at Regatta time. Nearby is the Stewards' Enclosure and a grandstand, where the élite in their summer finery revive the atmosphere of Edwardian England. Behind the enclosure are temporary car parks amid green fields; here, at lunch time, hampers emerge from car boots and champagne, strawberries and delicacies from Harrods or Fortnum and Mason are consumed in great quantities.

The racing takes place on the long, straight stretch of river to the north of Henley. Meanwhile, steamers, elegant Edwardian motor launches and boats laden with festive parties cruise along, watching the races. Despite the melée of boats and people the races take place without mishap and a good time is usually had by all at this most summery of all English celebrations.

As a break from the racing, there are other lovely places to enjoy nearby.

Left: Club balconies and sleek motor launches are crowded at the Henley Regatta finishing post, near Henley Bridge and the famous Leander Club.

Below: A village of hospitality marquees lines the banks of the Thames at Henley during the Regatta which is a notable social as well as sporting occasion.

Cowes on the Isle of Wight plays host to international yachtsmen during the week when the Solent, between the island and the mainland, becomes the centre of attention for everyone who likes to 'mess about in boats'.

Marlow, with its white suspension bridge, riverside church and famous Compleat Angler Hotel lies down river; to the north is Greys Court, a fine Tudor mansion set among the Chiltern Hills. Upstream the river winds through Sonning and its islands, past the industrial town of Reading, where Oscar Wilde once languished in gaol, and the splendid Tudor mansion of Mapledurham, then Pangbourne, near which lies Basildon House.

Another waterborne festival which has always been closely associated with royalty is Cowes Week, which takes place on The Solent, off the Isle of Wight. The Solent is overlooked by Osborne House, a favourite residence of Queen Victoria, whose husband, Prince Albert, gave the first Royal support to the week of yacht racing at Cowes.

The Isle of Wight stands offshore from Portsmouth and is a popular rendezvous for yachtsmen all year round. There are numerous charming

villages around its coast, like Bembridge and Freshwater, with harbours forested with swaying masts and peopled with busy amateur sailors making their boats shipshape or competing in club races. There are seaside resorts on the eastern side of the island at Sandown, Shanklin and Ventnor. Inland, the Isle of Wight is full of charm. Newport is the principal town, situated on the River Medina. About a mile away is Carisbrooke Castle, where Charles I was imprisoned.

The Cowes Regatta originally took place off East Cowes but now West Cowes is the centre of activity – especially around the exclusive Royal Yacht Squadron and the Island Sailing Club, whose members represent the best of British yachting. During Cowes Week the streets of the town are crowded with people who merely mess about in boats as well as with those who take yachting very seriously indeed. It becomes almost impossible to find parking or mooring spaces and hotels and restaurants are difficult to get into unless reservations have been made. If the weather is fine, there is no more splendid a sight than that of the Solent full of sails, especially when conditions call for the colourful spinnakers which balloon out over the sparkling blue water like exotic flowers. Poor weather does not dampen the enthusiasm of competitors, however, for winning at Cowes is a challenge that warms the blood. The races start at 10.30 every morning and include the Britannia Trophy and the New York Yacht Club Challenge Trophy.

The evenings at Cowes are given over to leisure and relaxation and there are social gatherings at all the clubs and pubs. Towards the end of the week balls are held, at which spectators and yachtsmen alike can enjoy the kind of fashionable social gathering first made popular when Prince Albert and, later, Edward VII took part in the Cowes races, just as Prince Philip and the Prince of Wales do today.

With their spinnakers billowing yachts make a magnificent and colourful spectacle as they compete in the races during Cowes Week.

An exciting moment in the Queen's Cup polo match. This fast equestrian game probably originated among the horsemen of the ancient Persian Empire.

Records of British involvement with horse-racing date back to the time of Richard II and the evolution of what might be called team sports in the tournaments between medieval knights. There is one team game, however, which emerged from the British relationship with India. This is polo – a four-a-side contest on a ground 274.32 m (300 yds) by 182.88 m (200 yds) – often regarded as an élitist sport reserved for the extremely rich or members of the Cavalry. While this may be true to some extent, for keeping a string of polo ponies is a luxury that most cannot afford, there has nevertheless been an increase in the numbers of spectators at this fast, exciting spectacle, which takes place on Smith's Lawn in Windsor Great Park during the summer.

The game probably originated in Persia in about 600 B.C. when the tribesmen of the Steppes began the centuries-long infiltration of the ruling empires of the day. It was natural that a people who moved about and fought on horseback should have evolved a competitive game which would demand the highest standards of horsemanship, audacity and fitness from the participants. It was also natural that the British Army, which depended on horsemanship for its command of foreign fields, should have also encouraged such a sport. The game was played by the British in India from the earliest days of their commercial settlements, and was imported to England in 1871, when a match was held at Hounslow between the 9th Lancers and the 10th Hussars. The founding of the Hurlingham Club gave the game further impetus, and the British interest

in polo carried it to other parts of the world. It was introduced in America in 1870 by Gordon Bennett, the son of a Scottish emigrant, who founded the *New York Herald*. A little later it arrived in Argentina, the country which has become the world's leading polo-playing nation and winner of international championships. The Argentinians were quick to realize the potential of their tough and hardy little Criollo horses, and set about breeding the perfect polo pony.

The game played at Smith's Lawn provides a stirring spectacle on a fine summer day, and interest is often heightened by the presence of the famous among participants and spectators. Prince Charles is a frequent player. The game is watched from a stand or from cars parked around the ground. The scene is as typically British as Henley and Ascot, with hampers of food being produced between games (chukkas). During the interval, spectators are invited to walk on the ground and replace or stamp in divots which have been thrown up by the horses' hooves.

Though much smaller in size than other equestrian events, the Smith's Lawn Championships present a revealing and colourful vignette of British life, best seen at the July International Polo Day. Other places where polo can be watched are Cirencester Park and Cowdray Park in Sussex.

GENTLEMEN AND PLAYERS

Until fairly recently, the notion was held that sportsmen could be divided into two groups; those who played for the fun of the game, and those who played for money. Although both types of players took part in matches, they did so under different conditions, with different entry gates and different changing rooms; their differences in social class were made obvious by the terms in which they were described – gentlemen and players. In recent decades, however, attitudes have changed, particularly in the very English games of cricket and tennis, due to the increase in professionalism and the levelling out of the class system.

In England, summer without tennis or cricket would be unthinkable and, as soon as weather conditions and the state of the grass become suitable, thousands of people book their courts at local tennis clubs and begin to turn up for games of cricket on club pitches and village greens.

A typical English scene in summer with white-clad cricketers on the village green. The competing teams usually represent clubs formed by towns, villages, or business houses.

The larger-than-life celebrities who play on the Wimbledon courts or Test Match pitches dominate newspaper headlines and conversations throughout the summer months.

Wimbledon is the major event of the summer tennis season and is held in June at the nostalgically named All England Lawn Tennis and Croquet Club. Originally, tennis was a game played by royalty and their entourage. The old form of the game, played on an indoor court like the one at Hampton Court, still exists, though it is now called Real Tennis to differentiate it from Lawn Tennis, the more popular form of the sport. Lawn tennis as we know it today began in the Victorian era, when its connection with croquet was more obvious; both these games were suitable for playing in a private garden with a well-tended lawn.

It is thought that lawn tennis was first played in the English Midlands where a Major Gem and his Spanish friend, Señor Perera, set up a club at Leamington Spa in 1872. The setting out of rules and regulations was due, however, to a Major Wingfield who marked out an hour-glass shaped court at a Christmas party in Nantclwyd, Wales and laid down the rules of

In these attractive grounds of the Wimbledon Lawn Tennis and Croquet Clubs the world's most famous players have competed since tennis competitions began in 1877.

A sunny day at Wimbledon stimulates an appetite for a bowl of traditional strawberries and cream.

play. Having patented his court and game, which he called Sphairistike, Major Wingfield set about converting the public to his new leisure pursuit. The game really took off when the Marylebone Cricket Club took an interest and designed a new rectangular court and appropriate rules to go with it. This new court and its regulations were adapted for the first Wimbledon Championship, which was held in 1877 in order to raise funds for the club. The Trophy, which was competed for by just 22 players that year was presented by *The Field* magazine, a publication which lent its support to the propagation of the new sport.

At first, lawn tennis was a genteel affair suitable, as Major Wingfield had claimed, for ladies as well as gentlemen and services were performed underarm. Like croquet, the game filled a need for the increasing numbers of middle-class society who were casting around for leisure time amusements which could serve as the focus for social gatherings. Two years after the first championship at Wimbledon, the overarm service was introduced and a new set of rules was drawn up by Mr. A. T. Myers. A further improvement was made in 1882, when the net was lowered, making it possible to hit the ball hard and low in the style perfected by modern players.

In the first decades of lawn tennis, the winners at Wimbledon were largely British but, gradually, the game spread to other countries, with the competition from abroad bringing about an improvement in technique. In 1900 the U.S.A. challenged Britain to a competition to be called the Davis Cup, which they won. Meanwhile the game of tennis had spread to France, Australia and New Zealand. By the 1920s lawn tennis had developed a huge following and the players were beginning to achieve the star quality which they possess today. A big name player of the time was Bill Tilden, a tall American with a cannonball service and a dramatic style on court that set the pattern for players to come. Among the women were Suzanne Lenglen, a French player who aroused crowd emotion by the grace and ferocity of her game and Helen Wills Moody, who won the Wimbledon singles title eight times. Heroes of the period between the wars were Britain's Fred Perry, the Frenchmen Henri Cochet, Jean Borotra 'the bounding Basque', Jean René Lacoste and Jacques Brugnon, and the Australian, John Crawford. Crawford's attempt to take the Grand Slam of the four major titles of Champion of Britain, France, the U.S.A. and Australia was foiled by Tilden.

Today, Wimbledon is still the world's senior lawn tennis event and the most colourful social gathering on the tennis calendar. Weeks before the tournament opens the Wimbledon courts are assiduously tended and a city of gaily decorated marquees is erected to accommodate the guests of commercial companies, who entertain their customers and associates with salmon, champagne and strawberries. Apart from the Centre and No. 1 Courts, all Wimbledon matches can be watched from the footpaths that intersect the courts. There is a great deal of movement from court to court as spectators follow their favourite players or move on to courts where particularly exciting matches are taking place. Wimbledon has an easy-going holiday atmosphere which is especially marked in the open area outside the Centre Court, near which the club restaurant is situated, and stalls dispense all kinds of refreshment as well as the inevitable strawberries and cream – Wimbledon's favourite dish. Among the melée of people there are glimpses of the players themselves as they come off court and return to the dressing rooms – though Centre Court finalists usually arrive in huge limousines, sweeping imperiously through the gates where hopeful visitors queue for tickets.

Rivalling Wimbledon as a typically English occasion is a Test Match played at Lords Cricket Ground. The headquarters of the game of cricket,

Lords is situated in north London, on the edge of the elegant residential areas of St. John's Wood and Hampstead; nearby is Regent's Park, headquarters of the London Zoological Society and home of London Zoo. When the game was first played at Lords the ground was surrounded by countryside, and places like Hampstead and Highgate were small villages where rich Londoners built country houses. Today, though submerged in the Greater London metropolis, these fashionable suburbs still retain a village atmosphere. Large areas of parkland remain at Hampstead Heath and Highgate Woods, commanding fine views over London.

The origins of cricket are not recorded, but it is probable that the sport evolved from a country game in which one player threw an object at a target and another tried to prevent it from landing. By the 18th century this pastime had become a game with rules and a defined area of play. A rudimentary club had evolved into the straight-sided bat we use today. The stumps had also acquired their present form, though before 1776 there were only two stumps supporting a single bail.

Like most country sports, cricket was a vehicle for gambling and bets were placed on the teams as well as on individual performers. This eventually led to corrupt practices, as players were tempted to 'throw' the match for pecuniary rewards. Gambling on cricket came to an end when the game was taken up by the English public schools, where it was looked upon as a means of friendly competition and not as a source of personal gain. The standard of play engendered by the schools was seen to be as good as, and even to exceed, that of 'professional' players and the betting aspects of the game were slowly replaced by an enthusiasm for the skill of teams and players for their own sake. The trend was encouraged by the foundation of the Marylebone Cricket Club in 1835, which laid down a code of conduct for a game which was now played all over the country.

Lords cricket ground in north London has been the scene of many a cricket Test Match and until recently was the only home of the cricket World Cup which is played every four years.

Overleaf: The oldest cricket club in the world, the Marylebone Cricket Club, has its headquarters at Lords, named after its founder Thomas Lord.

In 1886 a major innovation was the introduction of overarm bowling. This change in style and pace, together with the definition of the pitch by boundaries and the improvement in the quality of grounds, brought to the game the high degree of sporting skill displayed by such cricketing heroes as W. G. Grace, the bearded batsman who scored 126 centuries in his long career, Pilch of Norfolk, another great batsman, and Lillywhite of Sussex, a superb bowler nicknamed 'Nonpareil'.

The high point of the British cricket calendar is the series of Test Matches played against Australia, India, Pakistan, New Zealand, the West Indies and Sri Lanka. The contest began in 1877 when England played Australia at Melbourne. On this occasion England lost and such was the shock that *The Sporting Times* wrote an obituary which led to the 'cremating' of the wickets and bails used in the match. This led to the yearly battle between England and Australia for 'The Ashes', which still continues today.

The atmosphere at Lords on a Test Match day in summer is electric. The queues form early at the gates to the stands. Spectators fill the grandstand, which contains the Memorial Gallery of cricketing souvenirs, and others patronize the Warner Stand, named after the celebrated Sir Pelham Warner, where the media boxes are situated. Members of the Marylebone Cricket Club do not need to queue. They have access to the Long Room, above the Pavilion, from which they can survey the 2 hectares (5 acres) of the cricket field.

The match begins with a formal coin-tossing ceremony and then the winning captain can choose whether his team will bat or field first. This decision – which can be a fateful one – is reached after serious consideration of the weather and the condition of the pitch. After the toss, the fielding team is sent into position by the leading bowler and the two opening batsmen – bright and shining as two knights in their pads and gloves – stride out to their respective ends of the pitch.

Unlike the crowds found at football matches, cricket spectators do not usually launch into songs or slogans. Nevertheless, they are not backward in expressing their opinion on the way the match is progressing. Because of the subtlety of the game, strategy and tactics play a large part in team performance, and there are many opportunities for the crowd to voice their disagreement with the captain or individual members of the team; and there is an outcry if it is considered that the umpire has made a wrong

The golf course at Muirfield near Edinburgh was the course used for the British Open Championship in 1987. This glorious view from the 5th hole is across the Firth of Forth.

decision. On the whole, however, cricket supporters are a civilized and friendly crowd and, when the crowd includes supporters of teams like the West Indians, everyone can be sure of having an entertaining as well as an interesting day out – and one that can be memorable as a slice of British life at its best.

A sporting event which attracts the attention of sports fans all the world over is the British Open Golf Championship. The event was inaugurated at Prestwick in 1857 and was shared with the Royal and Ancient at St. Andrews for many years. Today the event takes place at one of several golf courses on different years.

Until 1857 competitions were generally limited to club members and the annual competition inaugurated at Prestwick and St. Andrews was an innovation. The success of this scheme led Prestwick to put up an award for the competition in 1860 and this is now regarded as the milestone date for the Open. Eleven years later St. Andrews offered the silver claret jug, and this is the trophy for which the world's leading golfers still compete.

Today St. Andrews, where the first rules of the game were written down in 1754, is still considered as the ruling authority on the game and the dream of every golfer is to play there at least once. The course used for the Open is known as the Old Course which has some of the most testing holes

The Royal and Ancient, the world's senior golf club, has four courses at St. Andrews. In this picture Ballesteros is seen on the old course which starts from the Royal and Ancient Club House.

As horsemen ride the borders at Langholm, Scotland, in a traditional ceremony along the English border, men cut and turn the soil to mark the frontier.

in the world. During any tournament held here, and especially in an Open year, the crowds follow the golfers round from hole to hole.

The town is crowded with visitors at Championship time and indeed at most competition times during the summer, for it is a pleasant holiday centre for the exploration of the Fife peninsula, which contains many historic sites, including Falkland Palace, favourite seat of the Scottish court under James V, Loch Leven Castle, where Mary Queen of Scots escaped from her imprisonment and Wemyss Castle, where she met Lord Darnley.

SUMMER IN THE COUNTRY

An unusual series of equestrian events takes place along the borders of Scotland and England during the summer. These are the Common Ridings which have been a tradition since 1816. The origins of the custom of Riding the Common lies in the time when boundaries were ill-defined and frequent arguments took place as to their exact delineation. Over 200 years ago at Langholm, a disagreement about boundaries led to an action in the Court of Session in Edinburgh in which it was decided that the legal rights of the Burgesses of Langholm obliged them to clearly define the boundaries by cairns and beacons and to walk or ride round the boundaries once a year, to repair marks and report encroachments.

At Langholm the Common Riding features certain strange objects carried in the procession round the boundaries. The first of these is the barley bannock and salted herring which symbolize certain old baronial

privileges and fishing rights. Then there is the spade, used for making the boundary and third is the thistle, the emblem of Scotland, but also, because of its spiky head, a warning to strangers not to interfere with the Riding and the Fair that is part of the entertainment. Finally, there is the floral crown, whose meaning is obscure but which may have stood for a gesture of loyalty to the Crown. In Langholm rosettes are worn in the colours of the winners of the Epsom Derby though the reason for doing so is shrouded in mystery.

The four original Common Riding towns are Langholm, Hawick, Selkirk and Lauder, all of them in the lovely valleys that lie along the Scottish border. Langholm is a mill town, where the rivers Esk, Ewes and Wauchope meet. Eskdale is a particularly attractive valley with its stream flowing westwards to the Solway Firth. To the west of Langholm is Hermitage Castle, a solid four square block standing in splendid isolation by Hermitage Water. It was here that Mary Queen of Scots visited Bothwell when he was wounded in an affray with the English, and rode from Jedburgh to do so.

Hawick is a large busy town attractively situated at the point where the rivers Slitrig and Teviot meet. It is a centre for the Scottish manufacture of woollens, tweeds and hosiery. It was here that the town youths ('callants') defeated the English in 1514, an event featured in the Hawick Common Riding. The English had their revenge by completely destroying the town in 1570. In the High Street is an equestrian statue to the 'callants' of Hawick which bears their ancient war-cry.

Riding or walking round boundaries was a way of establishing territorial rights. In Richmond, Yorkshire, the ritual of walking the 16 miles around the town is observed every seven years, the next occasion being 1990.

Another way of establishing boundary rights was to beat the bounds with a stick during a walk along them. This custom is still carried on in Oxford in the parish of St. Mary the Virgin on Ascension Day.

Selkirk was a royal Scottish burgh with textile mills built away from the town's tranquil centre where Sir Walter Scott, county sheriff for 33 years, is commemorated by a statue, as is Mungo Park, the explorer. Another memorial, of a man-at-arms, honours the townspeople who fought at Flodden and commemorates the capture of an English flag, kept in the library and paraded during the Common Riding, in which more than 300 riders participate.

Lauder lies to the north of Selkirk and the Walter Scott country where Abbotsford, Scott's house, and Dryburgh Abbey are situated. Unlike the Ridings of other towns, which have some warlike connections, Lauder's is simply a quiet ride round the boundaries. Unlike the others, the Lauder Riding has not happened continuously, for it was stopped between 1841 and 1911.

The Ridings are a popular event in which families take part and they have a festival air with pipe bands, children's parades, fair grounds, horse-racing and Highland dancing.

Some of the most glorious festivals of the summer take place in the country. In the days when Britain was an agricultural country, ruled by a rural economy, country festivals provided an opportunity for country people to get together for business and pleasure. At these fairs deals were made over produce, workers were hired, cattle and sheep bought and sold and, according to legend, wives were auctioned! Needless to say, these country festivals were occasions for merrymaking as well as work and a great deal of eating, drinking and dancing took place. Fairground operators would put up their stalls and people could see a bearded lady or Siamese twins, have their fortunes told, or accept the challenge of fairground bruisers to 'last a round for a pound'. Today, some of the lusty Rabelaisian character of the country shows has disappeared, but the

tradition of the country fairs continues all over Britain in the summertime.

The largest of the country shows takes place at Warwick, deep in the heart of England. At one time the powerful barons who ruled over vast areas of fertile land in this region became rich enough to challenge the King. Centuries later, industry put down its roots around the great Midland city of Birmingham and its neighbouring towns, and the area became known as the Black Country. Today, the black aspect of industry has faded under modern methods of manufacture, and the remaining countryside has returned to its former fresh glory.

Warwick has a great medieval castle on the banks of the River Avon, and still retains many Tudor and Georgian buildings as well as a group of 14th-century buildings named Lord Leycester's Hospital.

The castle lies by the River Avon in grounds that stretch up to the town's Castle Lane where there is a fine timbered house that once belonged to Thomas Oken, Warwick's 16th-century bailiff. To the north of the house is St. Mary's church which dates back to pre-Norman times, though the

Warwick Castle sits on a sandstone bluff above the River Avon. In 1978 the present Earl sold the castle, one of the finest in Europe, and it is now maintained as an historic home open to the public.

present building was rebuilt after a fire in 1694. The pride of the church is the Beauchamp chapel in which are the tombs of many members of the families that owned the castle, including that of the founder Thomas Beauchamp and of Robert Dudley, Earl of Leicester, favourite of Elizabeth I. He was given the castle when the Beauchamp line ceased.

In the countryside to the north of Warwick is the small village of Stoneleigh, once the home of a great Cistercian Abbey and later an 18th-century manor house in the Italian style, in whose grounds is held the most important and largest agricultural show in Britain.

The Royal Show of the Royal Agricultural Society of England set up its permanent residence at Stoneleigh in 1963 but the Society itself dates back to 1838 when it was founded to provide agricultural education to the nation's farmers. The Royal Show was the means by which new

A view over the part of the 102.2 hectares (250 acres) of grounds of the Royal Agricultural Society at Stoneleigh, Warwickshire, during the Royal Show.

technologies and farming achievements could be exhibited yearly and for over a hundred years it moved from place to place throughout England. Eventually it grew so large and complex that a permanent home had to be found to accommodate the 40 hectares (100 acres) of working machinery, 7000 livestock, 1300 exhibitors and over 1000 trade stalls that make up the show today. Work at the centre goes on throughout the year, however, and many other agricultural and equestrian societies also operate from the National Agricultural centre.

The exhibits at the Royal Show cover every aspect of modern farming both in the United Kingdom and abroad. In the special overseas section special attention is given to the agricultural problems of the Third World, where volunteers sponsored by the Society work throughout the year.

On the home front the various problems and changes in farming

There is plenty to see at the Royal Show which contains 40.5 hectares (100 acres) of working machinery, 1000 trade stands and over 7000 animals presented by some 1300 exhibitors.

methods are reviewed, with special emphasis on the new computer technologies available to farmers and the ancillary activities by which farmers can increase their revenue such as country sports meetings, farm holidays and the creation of a range of local food specialities.

Though essentially a show for farmers the Royal Show attracts over 160,000 visitors, many of whom have a general interest in country life and who are catered for by a programme of entertainments and side shows. The centre of entertainment is the Grand Ring where horse shows take place, attended by well-known riders of the show jumping and riding world. There are also coaching marathons, pet shows, steam engine exhibitions and demonstrations, Inter-Hunt Relay events, sheepdog trials and displays by members of the Armed Services.

The Royal Show represents the widest aspects of British farming and is the national show of the year but there are also many other shows of national and regional interest held throughout the country. Among these the Great Yorkshire Show ranks high among the county shows. The present show, held at Harrogate, covers some 40 hectares (100 acres) and includes two show rings where some of the finest livestock in Britain go through their paces for a large and admiring crowd.

The Show lasts for three days and attracts over 100,000 visitors who enjoy the many attractions which include show jumping by some of Britain's leading riders, and a large variety of demonstrations of the working and leisure activities of country life.

The pleasure of county shows lies not only in the shows themselves but in the opportunity they present for the exploration of the lovely countryside in which they take place and of which they are a focal point. In this respect the Great Yorkshire Show is particularly fortunate for it lies to the north of the industrial belt and on the fringes of the Yorkshire Dales, a

Left: Special events for young riders
are a popular feature of the Great
Yorkshire Show.

Below: A view of the cattle judging
in the grounds of the Great
Yorkshire Show.

Rosedale runs for 7 miles through the North Yorkshire moors. In the centre of the green valley lies the village of Rosedale Abbey but there is little left of the original monastery save a few stones by the village church.

680-mile-square national park of mountains and moorland crossed by broad pastoral valleys.

Harrogate itself is a charming town which became famous as a spa during the 19th century. The buildings erected during the spa's heyday are still there and give the town a Victorian character enhanced by the large areas of parks and gardens in which visitors to the spa used to take their constitutionals. Among the outstanding architecture is that of the Royal Pump Room which was built over the spring known as the 'Stinking Spaw' because of its sulphurous waters, and the Royal Baths, the largest hydrotherapy centre of the 19th-century world.

To the north of Harrogate stretches the Vale of York into which flow the rivers of the Yorkshire Dales on which lie some of the most historic Yorkshire towns and cities. Knaresborough to the north-east overlooks the River Nidd, its slopes crowded with Georgian houses above which are the ruins of a 14th-century castle and below which are caves where dripping water petrifies objects hung under their roofs. Mother Shipton, the famous prophetess, lived in one of these in the 15th century and forecast the invention of the aeroplane.

Further north on the River Skell is Fountains Abbey, a beautiful ruined monastery amid the trees of Studley Park, and nearby is the cathedral city of Ripon, whose narrow streets of old houses lead to the market square where the city Wakeman still blows his horn every evening at nine o'clock, a ritual known for a thousand years as Setting the Watch.

To the east of these towns the land rises to the Pennines, a wild lonely

area favoured by walkers and those who appreciate the great open spaces that still remain in Britain.

Among agricultural shows, the Royal Welsh Show stands out for the beauty of its setting and the particularly Welsh character of many of the exhibits and events. These take place under the auspices of the Royal Welsh Agricultural Society at Llanelwed, Builth Wells, which lies on the River Wye among the mountains of mid Wales. In its early life Builth Wells was a hotly contested strong point in the Wye Valley and possessed first a Norman and then a Plantagenet castle, but by the time of Elizabeth I these had been destroyed and today only the mound on which the castles stood remains. Later Builth Wells became a market centre and in the 19th century a spa.

Its market connections and central situation make it an appropriate place for a show that represents the best in Welsh agriculture and animal raising as well as other country activities. The Royal Welsh Show takes place on a special site, its permanent home, to the north of the town. The ground covers an area of 72.8 hectares (180 acres) and contains a main ring and two additional rings where competitions and judging take place. The trade stands, covering every branch of agriculture, occupy a large area and there are special sections where horses, cattle, sheep, dogs, pigs, fowls and other animals are housed and can be inspected by visitors. There is also an exhibition hall and sports area and all the usual catering facilities for an important exhibition that attracts some 150,000 visitors.

The horse and horsemanship part of the show is always a popular

Green fields and woods rise to the higher ground of the Cambrian mountains at Builth Wells, a pretty town once renowned as a spa.

feature, with some 37 different breed championships and events. Among these are the finely built thoroughbred Arabs, strong hunters, powerfully built Shires, the elegant Palominos and the tough little Welsh Cobs and ponies. The events are always full of excitement and include show jumping in all its various forms, children's events, pony trekking demonstrations, and various driving events in which drivers show off their skill at handling various types of vehicle over set courses at top speed. Of a more tranquil nature is the Concours d'Elegance, when smartly turned out vehicles and

Above: Sheep and sheepdogs play an appropriately important role at the Royal Welsh Show at Builth Wells which is situated on the River Wye.

Right: A champion looks aloof at the photographer but his companion proudly holds aloft his charge's trophy won at the Royal Welsh Show, Builth Wells.

drivers recall the days before the smell of exhaust fumes and mass-production cars.

In the cattle section there is also much variety, though the bulky creatures that provide meat for the markets do not lend themselves to active events; sheep do, however, and appear as a kind of woolly *corps de ballet* in the sheepdog trials. Watching a black and white border collie at work is one of the most satisfactory pleasures of life in the hilly counties. The intelligent and skilled dog working on its own initiative, but also

responsive to its handler's commands, makes an exciting spectacle which rivets the attention of the crowds as the dog drives a flock of sheep along a pre-set course. Then there is the tense moment as the dog attempts to separate two sheep from the rest without causing the whole flock to bolt. Finally the dog cajoles the sheep into a pen where his master waits to close the gate and to congratulate his partner on his performance.

Other exhibitions of canine skill and intelligence are seen in the main ring at gun dog demonstrations and when police dogs show off their talent for aiding the fight against crime.

In addition to the animal exhibits and demonstrations the Royal Welsh Show has a fine programme of country pursuits and at various times and places in the showgrounds one can watch the experts casting flies on to water with a dexterity in handling rod and line that provides absorbing watching. Other experts demonstrate sailing techniques for small boats and yet others show off their archery skills. There are also competitive cycle and motorbike sports which provide plenty of thrills and spills.

For the mechanically- or practically-minded there are hours of amusement at the stands where exhibits of every type of farming equipment are shown, and where the visitor can buy all kinds of merchandise, from souvenirs and food to do-it-yourself equipment and materials.

A county that still possesses much unspoiled landscape is Cornwall. Because of its barren nature, swept by Atlantic winds, Cornwall has not become an agricultural county, though some agriculture takes place in its sheltered valleys where the warm westerly air encourages the growth of early spring crops and flowers.

In the middle of Cornwall is an austere moorland where outcrops of rock rise among the ling and bracken; a magnificent and lonely place called

Brown Willy, at 400 m (1377 ft) the highest hill in Cornwall, rises above the wild stretch of Bodmin Moor seen here from Rough Tor.

Bodmin Moor, in the centre of which lies Dozmary Pool – yet another of the watery graves of King Arthur's Excalibur. In clear weather the views from this high plateau are magnificent, stretching to the Atlantic Ocean, the English Channel and the Bristol Channel, and the area is therefore popular with lovers of the open country. To the north, near the coast at St. Agnes, centre for the once profitable tin mining industry, is a patch of farming country where an unusual West Country event takes place. This is the West of England Steam Rally, a gathering of steam engines once used in farming as well as old fairground machines and vintage cars.

The steam rally is attended by steam rollers, farm engines, tractors, threshers, ploughing machines and all the glorious products of the fertile minds of engineers of the late Industrial Age. Here are none of the streamlined, characterless machines of the present but vehicles and engines which hover between practicality and art. Their design still speaks of an age of individualism when a machine was decorated with brass fittings, canopies, emblems and paintwork which gave it a personality of its own. It is hardly surprising that the owners of these splendid machines have a strongly personal relationship with their engines or that they personally bring them from hundreds of miles away by road to this gathering.

Cornwall is not an inappropriate place for this meeting of steam enthusiasts for Richard Trevithick, a Cornishman, was the inventor of the steam carriage and flanged wheel which proved that railway transport was a possibility.

The West of England Steam Rally takes place in August when the Cornish coastal resorts are crowded with holiday visitors, and the rally caters for those seeking entertainment as well as for steam buffs. There is a genuine old-fashioned fairground with steam-driven roundabouts, their

Old fashioned merry-go-rounds with hand carved and highly coloured horses are still major attractions at gatherings of steam-driven vehicles.

steam organs piping out familiar tunes, and steam swings looking like flying stage-coaches, as well as ferris wheels and all the fun of the fair.

Most of those attending the Steam Rally are also enjoying the beauty and excitement of the Cornish coast to the north and south. In the north the coast is rugged and the Atlantic breakers provide the waves needed for the surf riders who congregate at the sandy beaches of Perranporth and Newquay, the most popular resort which boasts no less than five beaches.

To the south the sea coast is gentler, with winding estuaries surrounded by green hills sheltering a myriad yachts, cruisers and dinghies that moor along their shores at resorts like St. Mawes, Falmouth, once the first base for the Atlantic packet boats, Flushing and other places on the estuary which stretches up to the cathedral city of Truro.

Perhaps among the most charming of the summer country fairs is the one held at Stratfield Saye, the home of the Duke of Wellington, to the south of the city of Reading.

The Wellington Show combines elements of Britain's military tradition with features of its country life. There are demonstrations by the Household Cavalry – one of the best-loved army units, with dazzling, romantic uniforms and splendid horses. Concerts by the Coldstream Guards and the Scottish Pipe Bands take place and, by way of contrast, exhibitions of parachute jumping by the Parachute Regiment.

The Wellington Show provides an opportunity to enjoy some of the oldest traditional activities of the British countryside. There are demonstrations of the rapidly disappearing craft of the farrier who, in the

Steam tractors prepare for the start of a race at a West Country steam rally, their paintwork glistening and brass fittings shining like gold.

days of horse-drawn transport, kept the horses shod and their feet in good order. As the blacksmith was the only man in the village to possess the equipment for working iron, his trade extended beyond the limits of a farrier's craft and blacksmiths became craftsmen who made iron gates for country estates and other iron implements and decorative work.

Another old-time occupation represented at Wellington is the breeding and training of falcons. These predatory birds were used for hunting and for sport in medieval times. Another hunter, the ferret, is also there, as they are used extensively in the country to control the rabbit population. Packs of beagles can be seen at the show. These small, tenacious hounds are used for hunting hares. Despite the opposition of the anti-hunting lobby the highly controversial sports of fox hunting, otter hunting, hare coursing etc. are still practised throughout Britain and are defended on the grounds that they are a part of the natural order of country life and contribute to the general well-being of the environment. Another and, some might say, more positive aspect of conservation is also seen at Wellington in the contribution of the Game Conservancy Trust, an association which conducts research into the habits of game and their vulnerability to disease.

Wellington Park and its house, Stratfield Saye, are situated in countryside typical of the south of England and a visit to the Wellington Show provides an opportunity to explore the surroundings. To the north is the Thames Valley; and to the west the North-West Downs, intersected by the River Kennet. On the banks of the Kennet lies Newbury, once a famous clothing town, trading in the wool from the sheep that grazed on the Downs. Today, the Downs are used for exercising race horses, especially at Lambourn to the north-west, beyond which lies the beautiful Vale of the White Horse. The Kennet also runs through Marlborough – one of the most attractive market towns in this part of England, with its broad, colonnaded main street. Its famous school has a burial mound within its grounds that is said to be the grave of Merlin, King Arthur's magician. Nearby, at Silbury Hill, a huge earthworks can be seen. Built about 2600

Above: A unit of the Household Cavalry sounds its trumpets to call attention to an event in the show in the grounds of Stratfield Saye, home of the Duke of Wellington.

Below: Among the many sporting activities in which visitors can participate at the Wellington Show at Stratfield Saye is clay pigeon shooting from butts made of straw bales.

B.C., this was once a fortress against marauding tribes. To the north of Silbury is another marvel, Avebury, where there is a vast megalithic stone circle of uncertain origin and date which John Aubrey, the 17th-century antiquary, considered more impressive than Stonehenge.

Another big country show which takes place in summer is the Chatsworth Game Fair in Derbyshire. Again, there is an emphasis on country pursuits. You can watch gun dog trials or horse-driving contests which have classes for farm carts, brewers' drays and dog carts, providing great enjoyment for drivers and spectators alike. Sheepdog trials, which have gained a wide audience since their first appearance on British television, are also a popular feature of the show. The skill and tenacity of the dogs and the uncanny understanding between dog and master serve as a reminder of some of the qualities of life that existed in Britain's agricultural past.

Chatsworth is particularly well suited as the site of a show which represents the finest traditions of English country life. The house is one of the finest Palladian buildings in Britain and has extensive grounds. The estate first came into the hands of the Cavendish family at the time of that formidable Elizabethan lady, Bess of Hardwick, the third wife of Sir William Cavendish. Mary Queen of Scots visited Bess at Chatsworth many times when that sad Queen was a prisoner in the care of the Duke of Shrewsbury, Bess of Hardwick's second husband.

Chatsworth lies on the southern fringe of the Peak District in Derbyshire, an entrancing region of steep limestone hills within the Pennine range and broken by the rivers Derwent and Dove. The countryside is a wonderland of peaks and valleys, vast underground caverns and beautiful gorges. In the centre of the Peak District lies Buxton, a spa where the healing waters still attract visitors. There is another spa at Matlock. One of the prettiest towns in the region is Bakewell and, nearby, is the fine manor house of Haddon Hall with its famous flight of steps down which, according to legend, Dorothy Vernon fled when eloping with Sir John Manners (ancestor of the present owner).

Both the Wellington and Chatsworth shows represent the old traditional country life of Britain, shared by landed gentry and countrymen; a life of common interests for both classes but one in which certain responsibilities were accepted on both sides in order to maintain the successful operation of the social system. Another kind of country gathering were the fairs and markets held for the benefit of local farmers, who came to buy and sell cattle, horses or produce. The horse fair, held at Appleby in the Vale of Eden, is one of these.

Today, Appleby Fair attracts the largest and most varied gathering of people of any country fair in England. Numerous groups of gypsies, traders, itinerant potters, tinkers and travelling market people pour in from all parts of Britain. For many of the participants the fair provides an opportunity for an annual reunion.

During the day, the business of the fair is transacted, with buyers vying with each other for the best horses. Harness races take place, to the excitement of spectators and gamblers who lay their bets with the bookies offering odds from their course-side stands. There are trotting races and other exhibitions of horsemanship. Besides the main spectacles of the fair, there is much to enjoy at Appleby – glimpses of horses being washed in the River Eden, small gipsy children playing, and fortune-tellers revealing the future to those who will cross their palms with silver.

Appleby lies on the west side of the Pennines, in the fertile Vale of Eden through which the Romans built a road joining the eastern and western sides of northern England. Deep valleys cut into the Pennines from the Eden towards the summits of Cross and Great Dun Fells. On its northward

These Cumberland and
Westmoreland wrestlers in their
distinctive costumes attempt to
down each other at the Grasmere
Sports.

Preceding page: The beauty of the
English lakes has inspired poets
and painters for countless years.
Here is a group of artists preparing
to paint Ullswater from Angle Tarn
Track.

course, the river reaches Penrith, an ancient town with a ruined castle and
Iron Age earthworks. Near Penrith lies Askham, one of the prettiest
villages in the region, and nearby is the impressive shell of Lowther Castle
set in a beautiful park. From here it is only a few miles to Ullswater, the
most easterly lake of the glorious English Lake District, the land of
Wordsworth and the lake poets. At Grasmere, also in the Lake District, a
great meeting is held in August for lakeland sports. The setting for the
sports is sublime, surrounded by the high summits of Helm Crag and Seat
Sandal to the north and the heights of Loughrigg Fell across Grasmere lake
to the south.

The sports take place in a field by the delightful village of Grasmere,
where Wordsworth lived before moving to Rydal Mount. They attract
thousands of spectators, both local inhabitants and tourists. The events
are testing affairs including races up the rough slopes of Helm Crag and
wrestling in Cumberland and Westmoreland styles. There are also hound
trails, in which hounds follow a scent across the fells. During the games the
village is even more crowded than usual with visitors, who fill the hotels
and pack into restaurants and bars where they are entertained with
traditional songs and country dancing. While in Grasmere, most visitors
pay their respects to the great lake poet, Wordsworth, who lived in the
cottage – now a museum – at Town End and is buried in the Grasmere
churchyard.

The Grasmere Sports provide an opportunity to explore this marvellous region of Britain which, though ignored throughout centuries of British life, became a much sought after 'Eden' during and after the period of Romantic literature which found in nature a new kingdom of spiritual revelation. Grasmere and its neighbouring lake, Rydal Water, are at the centre of Wordsworth country and well situated for the exploration of the mountainous core of the Lake District. Summits like Sca Fell and Great Gable offer breathtaking views of the lakes and their surrounding countryside. Wast Water and its barren screes stretch to the south and, to the west, is wooded Ennerdale Water. The two charming lakes of Buttermere and Crummock Water lie to the north-east, with quiet villages and steep mountains. To the north is Derwent Water, home of the lake novelist Hugh Walpole – a lovely, broad expanse of water with wooded islands. Thirlmere lies to the east, alongside Hellvellyn, and to the south is Windermere. The most popular lake of all, Windermere, with its large lakeside resort of Bowness, is the only really crowded place in this beautiful, peaceful region.

The fine old town of Alnwick, in Northumberland, is dominated by Alnwick Castle which for centuries has been the main stronghold of the powerful Percy family, whose head is the Duke of Northumberland. One of the Duke's more pleasant duties these days is to be president of Alnwick Fair, one of the most popular events of the Northumbrian summer.

For seven days, starting on the last Sunday in June, Alnwick has an extra liveliness as the fair, including a market and a host of entertainments, takes over the town. While this particular fair has only been taking place since 1969, it is part of a strong tradition, for Alnwick once had several big fairs every year, with one of them being held in June or July from the late 13th century right up to the 20th century.

Although parts of Lake Windermere become very crowded in the summer, it is still a place for leisurely relaxation as well as active water sports.

A specific historical theme is usually chosen for Alnwick Fair each year, so that visitors might encounter the costumes, trades, entertainments, stocks and ducking stool of medieval England one year and a re-creation of 18th-century life the next.

Whatever the theme, the fair always begins on the Sunday with a grand procession of bands, decorated floats, costumed riders, street entertainers and dancers, all led through the streets of the town by the Herald who has just proclaimed the fair in Alnwick Market Square in the presence of the Fair Queen and her retinue. After the procession, there is usually a Sedan Chair Race.

The Market Square is the hub of the fair, for this is where the market stalls are set up all week and where a temporary stage is the setting for a programme of events which includes singing, dancing, music-making, street theatre and other entertainments.

Above: Folk dancers and singers from all over the world perform at the Billingham, Teeside International Folklore Festival. This lively team of Spanish dancers delighted the crowds.

Opposite: One of the high spots of the day at Alnwick Fair, which has a different theme every year. This 'mock' sedan chair race celebrates the creation of the postal system in Queen Victoria's reign.

The Ould Lammas Fair at Ballycastle, County Antrim in Northern Ireland transforms the usually peaceful town into a lively market-place.

Though many fairs began as markets for livestock, few of them continue fulfilling this function and many of them have become funfairs. The Ould Lammas Fair in Ballycastle in Northern Ireland is an exception.

The fair was granted a charter in 1606 and its main business then was dealing in sheep. It took place at Lammas, a church festival whose name has given rise to some confusion, some people being under the impression that Lammas, because of its onomatopaeic association with the word lamb, describes a sheep fair. This is not so, however. Lammas is the feast of the imprisonment and liberation of St. Peter, and the name has no connection with sheep; the fact that the Ould Lammas Fair originally was a sheep fair is coincidental.

The evening before the fair is a busy time with much coming and going in the town of Ballycastle as the livestock are transported and driven about the town towards the livestock pens; some for cattle, others for horses and yet others for goats, sheep and other animals. In the Diamond, a square in the centre of the town, the traders start setting up their stalls in preparation for the morning, when they will be full of market produce, clothing, household wares and other merchandise, including the favourite local sweetmeat, Yellow Man (a kind of toffee coloured yellow), and another Ballycastle delicacy called Dulse, which is an edible seaweed which most people like to eat raw.

Throughout the day there is much dealing in livestock auctions and the 300 to 400 stalls in the market are thronged with buyers looking for bargains. The Ould Lammas Fair is very much a family occasion and for children there is a fun fair where they can ride roundabouts, slither down the slides and enjoy the swings, trampolines and other equipment in their special enclosure.

Perhaps because of its isolated situation facing the Mull of Kintyre at the

very north of the Antrim mountains, Ballycastle has a special character that endears it to all its visitors. One of these was the Italian inventor Marconi who first tried out his wireless system from Ballycastle to the offshore island of Rathlin. This charm still affects the visitors who arrive today to visit the unique formation of basalt columns along the coast to the west, the famous Giant's Causeway. Those who are fortunate enough to be in the area during the Ould Lammas Fair take away the memories of a rare occasion which was immortalized by John Macauley in his song, the

The strange Burryman that appears at South Queensferry, at the southern end of the Forth Bridge on the eve of the annual fair looks like a creature from another world.

137

chorus of which runs:

> At the Ould Lammas Fair, boys were you ever there?
> Were you ever at the Fair in Ballycastle Oh?
> Did you treat your Mary Ann to dulse and yellow man?
> At the Ould Lammas Fair at Ballycastle Oh.

A tantalizingly obscure celebration at South Queensferry in Scotland occurs in August, when a parade and fair are held and a beauty queen is crowned.

The fair dates back hundreds of years but became especially significant in the 17th century when Linlithgow, 8 miles to the west of Queensferry, challenged Queensferry's right to hold a fair and demanded that merchants selling their wares there should pay dues. When a Linlithgow customs officer attempted to collect these there was a riot and South Queensferry was fined for disturbing the peace. Later, however, the town appealed to the courts and in 1636 won the right to be named a Royal Burgh and free port.

Since then the annual fair has been celebrated with increased gusto; there is a parade with music, dancing, games and other entertainments throughout the day. The eve of the fair is marked by the appearance of the Burryman, a strange apparition who it seems is not historically connected with the fair but makes his mysterious visit to South Queensferry at this time. The Burryman is an extraordinary and sinister personage who suggests those powerful figures of the natural world represented in other parts of Britain by the Green Man and in mythologies by kings of the wood, satyrs and other supernatural creatures. The Queensferry Burryman is a weird creature, his body is made up entirely of burrs except for his hands and the yellow Scottish standard, with its lion rampant in red, across his middle. The burrs extend over his face but on his head he wears an extraordinary hat made of flowers. In each hand he carries a staff from which sprout magnificent bunches of hydrangeas. In this unwieldy outfit, aided by two assistants, the Burryman walks stiff-legged around

The Dunmow flitch, a piece of bacon, is presented by the jury seen in this picture to the couple they judge to be the happiest in the village.

After the jury has made its decision, the man and wife are carried round the village on a palanquin borne by eight stalwarts.

Queensferry and is welcomed by the people, who see him as a good omen and ply him with whisky. The Burryman's perambulations do not go unrewarded, for as he goes he collects money for charity, thus enabling everyone to participate in a ritual which perhaps affirms man's faith in nature and humanity.

A summer ritual whose roots go back to pre-medieval times is the one celebrated at Great Dunmow in June. This is a particularly meaningful occasion for married people, or those about to be married, as it is concerned with marital happiness. A flitch (side) of bacon is presented to the married couple who can swear on oath that they have not quarrelled or wished themselves single again during the past year and a day.

The tradition was probably started by the Lord of the Manor or the monks of the Augustinian Priory of Little Dunmow to encourage the institution of marriage. Exact information about its origins are unknown, though a written record of the event was made in 1445.

According to the records, applicants for the Dunmow Flitch had to go to the Priory where, kneeling on a hard and sharp-edged stone they swore to their happiness in the presence of the Prior and a congregation of monks and villagers from the estate. After judgment was made as to the most worthy couple, the man was carried round in a procession.

The ritual is carried out each leap year, and the next one will be in 1988. Today the ceremony is carried out more in fun than in earnest and is an excuse for much ribaldry and merrymaking. The present ceremony was revived at the instigation of the novelist Harrison Ainsworth in the 19th century, after having fallen into disuse. The lighter spirit of the revival was accompanied by the creation of entertainments to amuse the public at Dunmow Flitch time, with processions, games and sports. The previously

The girls in elaborate 'horse' costumes line up behind the boys at the Boy Ploughmen contest at St. Margaret's Hope, Orkney. There is a separate competition for the best groomed 'horse'.

serious judgment of the couples claiming the flitch has become a parody, with a mock judge and counsels who carry out a comic cross-examination to the amusement of the spectators who join in the general merriment.

The Dunmow Flitch ritual still attracts many visitors, for it takes place in a very rural part of Essex. Here the visitor can find many pretty villages, particularly in the valley of the Rodings, where an old Saxon track which gives the valley its name once ran. Great Dunmow stands at the northern end of the Rodings and is an attractive market town on the River Chelme. It was here that Lionel Lukin, the inventor of the lifeboat, tested his first models. Little Dunmow, where the ruins of the Priory still stand, lies to the east, in green wooded countryside. To the south, through narrow leafy lanes, lies High Roding, with its cottages and 13th-century church, and Leaden Roding, which has a fine old hall. There are eight Rodings altogether with such picturesque prefixes as Abbess, Beauchamp, Aythorpe, Berners, Margaret and White; the Rodings were the inspiration for villages in some of the novels of Anthony Trollope.

Another mysterious ritual takes place in the southern Orkney island of South Ronaldsay in August. The event involves young boys and girls of the tiny village of St. Margaret's Hope. Once an Easter festival, this unusual ploughing match now takes place on the third Saturday in August. Boys and girls parade on the Sands O'Right or some other sandy stretch if this is not convenient. The girls are dressed in elaborate costumes, the basis of which is a harness, horsecollar, bridle and other equine accoutrements. These are, however, highly decorated with flowers, ribbons, baubles, feathers, tassles, rosettes and anything else that has been saved up over the years. When all the girls have been decorated they are judged by a panel of experts who decide which has the most spectacular decorations and which the most workmanlike harness. A decision having been made, the girls'

part is over and the boys, who have been spectators until now, prepare for the ploughing contest.

This is carried out with miniature ploughs in wood and metal which have been carefully handcrafted and considered family treasures, preserved from generation to generation. The beach is now cleared and divided quickly into 'rigs', areas which the boys will plough with their miniature ploughs. The contest is conducted with great seriousness as the boys begin to walk up and down the rig, ploughing the straightest furrows that they are capable of. Some of the boys, impatient or full of irrepressible high spirits, go too fast and are soon out of the running, but others work with great intensity and dedication. There are six prizes: the big one is for the Best Ploughed Rig, the others for the best first furrow (the 'feering'), for the straightest furrows, for the neatest ends, the best finish and the first finished. After the judging everyone retires to partake of some refreshment to mark the occasion.

The significance of this strange ritual is lost in the mists of time; perhaps it is Norse in origin, for this archipelago of isolated islands was part of the kingdom of Norway at one time. Whatever its meaning, the ritual itself is as mysterious and fascinating as the islands on which it takes place and which attract many summer visitors. There is plenty to see: Kirkwall, the largest town, with its busy harbour, its fine St. Magnus Cathedral and its ruined palaces of Bishop and Earl; or the prehistoric monuments between Finstown and Stromness, which were built by unknown peoples later overcome by the Picts and the Norsemen who invaded the islands in order to eliminate the pirates who preyed on their shipping.

Today the Orkneys are a peaceful place with huge vistas of sea and sky and bird life which attracts ornithologists and amateur bird watchers from all over the world.

The boy ploughmen concentrate on making their furrows with miniature ploughs, oblivious to the crowds watching the championship.

Opposite: Nelson's flagship, the Victory is a focus point of many of the events that take place during Navy Days at Portsmouth, Hampshire.

THE MILITARY SHOWS

John of Gaunt's famous speech in Shakespeare's Richard II must be the most moving patriotic oration ever written. In it, the dying son of Edward III sums up the deep-rooted pride of a person for the country where he has been born and bred. He speaks of the sense of identity acquired through place and the spiritual pride of a wider order, based on Christian service and true chivalry, which are the inspiration of a true national spirit.

It is in this spirit that Britain celebrates many of the military festivals that occur throughout the year, making the shows put on by the Army, Navy and Air Force more of a festival than a display of military might. However, there is nothing of toy soldiers in the modern military face of Britain.

Britain's senior military service is the Royal Navy, founded by the Tudor king, Henry VII, who had the vision to realize that Britain's future depended upon strength at sea. The British naval tradition is a proud one and one which laid the foundations for navies the world over.

It is appropriate that one of the great naval festivals of the year should take place at Portsmouth, for the port is the home of two ships that represent famous moments in British naval tradition. One of these is the *Mary Rose*, the hull of a Tudor man-of-war, flagship of Henry VIII's fleet which was raised from its watery grave in 1985. The other is the *Victory*, the flagship at Trafalgar of Horatio Nelson, an admiral who not only established British supremacy at sea but became a model for the officer class of navies worldwide. As well as being open to visitors the *Victory* provides a splendid background to a *son et lumière* spectacle during Portsmouth Navy Days in August which evokes Portsmouth's glorious past. Portsmouth, one of Britain's major naval ports, is also the base for the Royal Navy's main gunnery school at Whale Island, the Torpedo and Anti-submarine school at land-based *HMS Vernon* and the submarine base at *HMS Dolphin*, across Portsmouth Harbour at Gosport.

Portsmouth began its naval connections in the reign of Henry VII, when a dry dock was established under Royal patronage and a fortress, ruined in the Second World War, was built. The port grew during Tudor and Stuart times, as England became increasingly involved in continental politics and in the struggle for control of the sea routes. Charles II, who was acutely aware of the maritime threat to England's trade, was very much interested in Portsmouth. Indeed, his wedding to Catherine of Braganza took place there. During the 19th century Portsmouth was a base for Nelson's Navy, which sheltered in its enclosed harbour and often lay at anchor in the Solent and in the lee of the Isle of Wight. In our own century, Portsmouth and the Solent were the scene of reviews of the most powerful navy in the world, filled with dreadnoughts, cruisers, destroyers and submarines, with their masts and lines fluttering with a myriad coloured signalling flags and pennants.

During Navy Days the dockyard receives over 100,000 visitors who are entertained by static displays of naval equipment and weaponry and practical demonstrations of the jobs the Senior Service carries out in the course of its duties, including deep-sea diving displays, salvage operations, the replenishment of ships at sea and marine raids in high-speed boats. One of the aspects of Portsmouth Navy Days most appreciated by the public is the opportunity to take trips on landing and other craft and to visit the aircraft carriers, cruisers, destroyers and submarines stationed at the naval base.

The festive atmosphere, enlivened by marine band marching displays, also spreads outside the dockyard to what remains of the old port after its Second World War bombardment which caused extensive damage. Here, by the remaining walls and towers of the fortress built by Henry VIII, there

Overleaf: All kinds of naval vessels gather at Portsmouth in August for Navy Days, a festival at the naval base where Charles II married Catherine of Braganza and from which Nelson embarked on the Victory before the battle of Trafalgar.

Goodwood on the Sussex Downs is usually thought of in connection with races such as the Goodwood Cup and Sussex Stakes but Goodwood House is renowned for dressage competitions.

is a cluster of small houses and pubs where some of the atmosphere of the days when Nelson's fleet was anchored in the Solent can be conjured up as one sips one's tot of rum.

Portsmouth is situated on a flat peninsula which extends eastwards, between the harbours of Portsmouth and Langstone, with further tidal harbours beyond as far as Chichester. This vast area of sheltered inlets is the paradise of yachtsmen of every type, from dinghy sailors to the captains of sleek ocean-going craft. Every village shows evidence of the local preoccupation with boats. Chichester itself, though only joined to the sea by a canal, is a city of people who take pleasure in the sea, and has fine restaurants, shops and a superb cathedral. Nearby, at Fishbourne, you can see one of the finest Roman villas in Britain.

Inland lie the downlands of West Sussex, a lovely rural area full of splendid houses and pretty villages. There is 14th-century Court House in East Meon, a lovely village on the river Meon where Isaac Walton, author of *The Compleat Angler*, fished. There is the ruined Bishop's Palace at Bishops Waltham and, near Petersfield, Uppark – the house where Emma Hamilton lived. Petworth House, where the artist Turner did some of his finest late works, is to the north-west, and Midhurst with the lovely Cowdray Estate is nearby.

Concorde sweeps over Yeovilton Royal Naval Air Station on International Air Day when aircraft from many nations are on show.

Another noteworthy village in the area, for those who want to combine the naval celebrations at Portsmouth with a visit to the shrine of cricket, is Hambledon. The local inn is called 'The Bat and Ball' in commemoration of the fact that the game of cricket was first played here, on the village green, in 1774. It is a fortuitous coincidence that Thomas Lord, first owner of Lords cricket ground, lived and died in the nearby village of West Meon.

North of Chichester is another sporting venue, Goodwood House and the Goodwood racecourse, which sits high on the Downs, with superb views of the coast.

Another great naval day that provides thrills and entertainment during the summer is held at the Royal Naval Air Station at Yeovilton near Yeovil. The Yeovilton International Air Day is designed to give the Royal Navy the opportunity to display its equipment and the skills of its personnel. There are displays by aircraft of the Fleet Air Arm, including Sea Harriers (commando assault versions of the Sea King helicopters), Canberras and Hunters. Other aircraft are on show – some from other countries such as France, Germany and the United States. In addition to air displays, Yeovilton Air Day includes demonstrations by Commandos, parachute units, and an exhibition of old aircraft like the Hurricane and the Catalina flying boat.

Yeovil is a market town which has grown into an industrial centre. It is still surrounded by beautiful countryside, however, where fine manor houses provide centres of interest for visitors. Montacute, one of the finest Tudor houses in England, lies to the west. Barrington Court, near Crewkerne, is also of the Tudor period. Hinton House, in the pretty village of Hinton St. George, is well worth visiting. To the east of Yeovil lies the charmingly named village of Compton Pauncefoot, so called because it

147

once belonged to a Norman knight, Compton, who was nick-named Paunch Fort owing to his stout belly. The village has a typically English 19th-century folly resembling a gothic castle. Nearby, a more authentic fortress rises on Cadbury Hill. The entrenched slopes around the plateau are alleged to be the site of Arthur's Camelot, but are more likely to be connected with King Alfred's desperate stand against the Danes in the 9th century. To the south of Yeovil lies a pilgrimage spot for admirers of the most compelling poet of the 20th century, T. S. Eliot. Eliot was inspired by the village of East Coker to write one of the poems of his Four Quartets.

The Army also has an opportunity to demonstrate its skills during the summer. This takes place indoors, in London, at the Royal Tournament – one of the most popular military shows of the year and one of the most colourful. The Tournament was first held in 1880 and grew in popularity when it began to include such exciting items as hand-to-hand combat and an event known as 'cleaving the Turk's head', in which mounted soldiers rode past an effigy of a person with a turban and tried to cut the head in two with their swords.

Left: Every year The King's Troop Royal Horse Artillery puts on a breathtaking display at the Royal Tournament.

Today, the Royal Tournament takes place over three weeks and concentrates on colourful, courageous and highly skilled displays by the Combined Services of the Army, Navy and Air Force which the public applaud with tremendous enthusiasm. There are also demonstrations by the Royal Horse Artillery, the police dogs of the Royal Air Force and the Massed Bands of the Royal Marines.

Of the outdoor military shows, perhaps the most splendid is the Edinburgh Military Tattoo, which takes place at Edinburgh's historic castle every evening during the Edinburgh International Festival in August. The castle crag has been occupied since Pictish times and became an outpost of the King of Northumbria in the 6th century. The Scottish King, Malcolm Canmore, lived in the fortress built by Edwin in the 11th century, and it continued to be a much fought-for prize during the centuries of warfare against the English. The warfare came to an end when James VI of Scotland, who was born in the castle, became James I of England.

The Long Esplanade in front of Edinburgh Castle is the arena for the

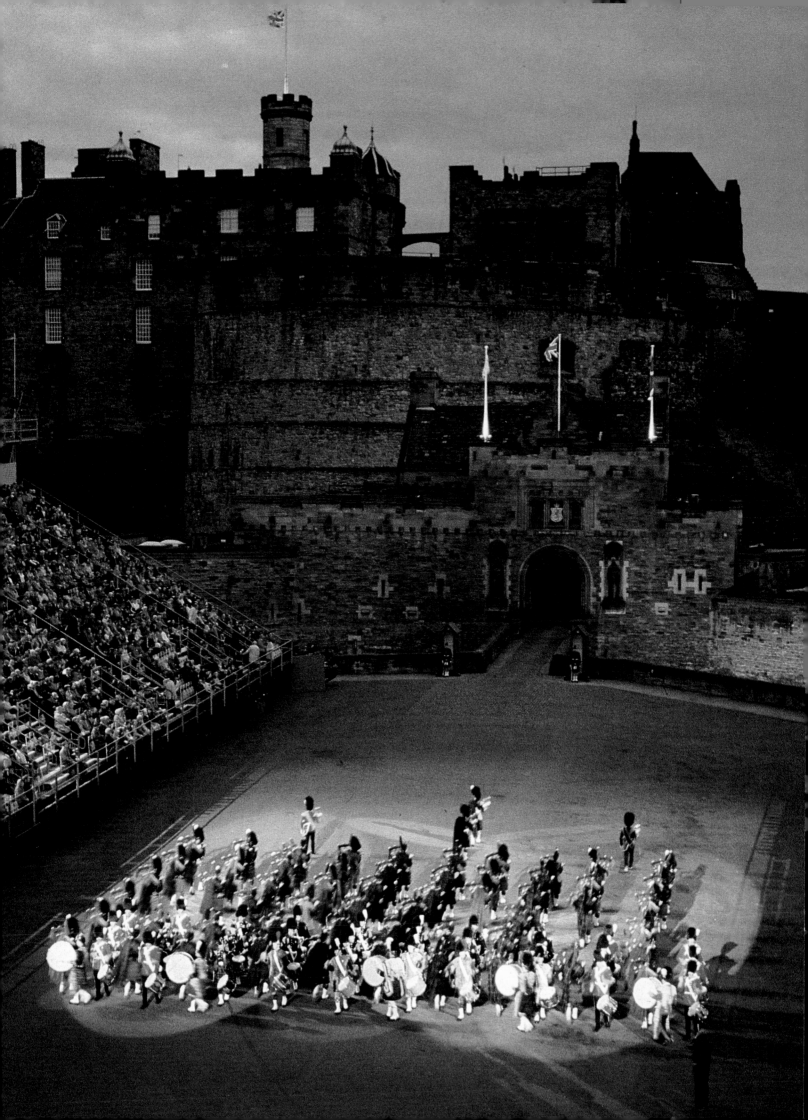

Edinburgh Tattoo. Stands are erected to accommodate the thousands of spectators who arrive to see the regiments and military units from all over the world. To the right of the Esplanade is the Witches Well, where 300 witches were burnt in the 15th century. At the upper end of the Esplanade is the castle itself, across the moat, flanked by statues of Scotland's heroes, Robert the Bruce and William Wallace. Inside the castle walls are Argyll's Tower, named after the Marquess of Argyll who was held there before his execution in 1661, and the regimental museum of the Royal Scots, the oldest infantry regiment in the British Army. On the top platform of the castle stands Mons Meg, an ancient cannon which was made at Mons and was probably used in the time of James II. The oldest part of the castle is St. Margaret's Chapel, built in the 11th century. Also within the castle precincts are the Crown Square, with the Crown Rooms where the Scottish Royal Regalia is kept, and the Queen's Apartments, which include the room where Mary Queen of Scots gave birth to James VI, and the Old Parliament Hall. From the castle there is a magnificent view over Princes Gardens and the old town with the Grassmarket and Greyfriars Churchyard, built on the site of a Franciscan Priory.

The Tattoo takes place in the evening and it is a wonderful experience to see the twilight sky overhead darken and the stars come out as the Tattoo, with its regimental bands, unfolds. As might be expected, there is a good deal of pipe music. The strangely stirring strains of the pipes have led many a regiment into battle in the past and still have the ability to move the crowd – even those who are not of Scottish ancestry.

FESTIVAL TIME

In June Scotland celebrates its most famous poet Robert (affectionately known the world over as Robbie) Burns at Ayr and Alloway.

Robbie Burns was born at Alloway in 1759 in the small cottage which his father built. He spent the first seven years of his life here and went to school at Alloway Hill, where he soon developed an interest in literature and the folk ballads. His enthusiasm for the songs of his homeland was encouraged by Betty Davidson, an old lady who lived in the Burns' home.

Though his interest in literary works developed early, Burns was no bookworm and he spent much of his spare time with the sailors and smugglers who frequented the Ayr inns and with the young women of the town who were bewitched by the romantic young poet. When his father died Burns took over the small family farm, but he had neither the money nor the vocation for an agricultural life and he was soon in financial trouble. At about this time he met the great love of his life, Jean Armour, a headstrong girl who nevertheless inspired him to write some of the finest love poems in any language. His love affair was stormy, and soon Burns was sufficiently discouraged to consider emigrating to Barbados. However, the publication of his poems in Dr. Johnson's *Scots Musical Museum* gave him encouragement. About this time he returned to his true love, Jean Armour, and married her, settling in another farm at Ellisland, which once again proved a failure. It was while here that he wrote 'Tam O'Shanter' the philosophical and ironic poem about Tam, who got drunk at the inn (now named after him) and rode to the Brig o' Doon where he was pursued by witches holding their black rituals in the local church.

This poem is today the inspiration for one of the most colourful features of the Burns Festival which is now linked to the Ayr Arts Festival. The Tam O'Shanter procession from Ayr to Alloway takes place in the evening and consists of a party representing Tam O'Shanter and his friends wearing the tartan and accompanied by pipes and crowds of well wishers. The procession starts from the Tam O'Shanter Inn in Ayr High Street.

Opposite: Massed pipe bands provide an impressive and memorable show at the Edinburgh Military Tattoo held within the walls of Edinburgh Castle.

Above: The Robbie Burns festival at Ayr includes a 'ceilidh' where people gather for songs and poetry. In summer these are often held in the open air.

Opposite: Bath Abbey rises above the splendid Roman Baths used between the 1st and 4th century and then falling into ruin until excavated in 1755.

The original Tam O'Shanter had been at the market all day and, as was usual, had drunk a good deal of whisky before setting off for home. When a storm arose he imagined he could see witches and all the hounds of hell around him. On arriving at Alloway he imagined he saw witches even in the church and among them a young and beautiful witch dressed in a short shift called a cutty sark. Calling out to her, Tam revealed his presence and was chased by the witches. Tam now rode over the old bridge over the Doon which the witches could not cross because it was over water, but the young witch managed to pull off his horse's tail.

The Tam O'Shanter ceremony is only one part of the Robbie Burns celebrations, which include a large number of activities, such as the traditional Scottish Ceilidhs or gatherings where singing, dancing and story telling are an essential element, as are the drams of whisky which loosen the tongue of even the most diffident participants. There is also a Fiddlers Rally where Scottish fiddlers compete with each other, cheered on by their supporters, a market selling a vast variety of items both regional and imported, a fun fair, dog shows, games and other contests of skill and chance. Music is an essential ingredient of the Burns Festival and concerts and band performances are included.

Musical festivals take place in Cheltenham and Bath. The Bath Festival incorporates the arts, theatre and fringe activities – some 70 shows altogether – held in the beautiful Georgian city and now extended, for some of the concerts, to Bristol. The core of Bath lies around its cathedral, which began its life in the 15th century and serves as a venue for some of the musical events. Bath has an elegance and style rare nowadays, and the little streets full of delightful shops, lit by candles burning in the windows of Georgian houses, provide wonderful strolls before and after concerts. The most splendid Roman Baths in Britain are in Bath and the adjoining

The present Abbey Church, begun in the 15th century, makes an impressive venue for concerts during the Bath Festival.

museum contains exhibits excavated from the baths. The therapeutic waters that delighted the Romans also brought the city popularity in the 18th century. It became a fashionable centre under the censorious eye of Beau Nash, and it owes its elegant architecture to this period. The main architects of the city were John Wood and his son. Together they erected buildings on Queen's Square, the Circus and the Royal Crescent and designed the Assembly Rooms, which house the Museum of Costume and are also used for festival concerts.

While the festival is on, there is great activity in Bath. Its excellent hotels and restaurants are well patronized and, in the streets, the fringe entertainers provide day-long amusement with dances, conjuring displays and busking. During its 17 days, the Bath Festival is a varied cultural feast; not only are there major concerts, theatre and art shows, but also jazz sessions, ballet, marionette theatre, literary meetings, lectures and all the fun of the fair.

A British musical event which runs throughout the summer months is celebrated at the little village of Glyndebourne in Sussex, amid the undulating landscape of the South Downs. At the eastern extremity of the Downs, near to the point where they plunge dizzily into the sea at Beachy Head, there is a Tudor mansion and, unexpectedly, an opera house created by Mr. John Christie in 1934. Few people could have foreseen that the almost foolhardy act of building of an opera house in the middle of the country would be a successful venture, yet Glyndebourne has become one of the world's most favoured opera venues. Mr. Christie's enthusiasm, together with the skill of Fritz Busch, Conductor of the Dresden State Opera, Rudolf Bing, Viennese musical impresario and Professor Carl Weber of Berlin, rapidly turned Glyndebourne into an internationally renowned summer opera centre, and also a social venue of distinction.

At Glyndebourne, the opera house is set in a beautiful and secluded garden, surrounded by meadows and open downlands inhabited only by cattle and sheep. The garden itself is an English delight, with box hedges, a croquet lawn, a tennis court and three lakes. Here the ducks swim with a hopeful eye on the opera-loving picnickers who sit elegantly, in their dinner jackets and evening dresses, around sumptuous hampers containing champagne, smoked salmon and other delicacies. This unlikely scene in today's workaday England is part of the magic show that Glyndebourne puts on for its visitors from the moment that a uniformed attendant helps them to park their cars, or a special bus meets the train from London, to the moment of departure when, after listening to a popular opera such as *Cosi fan tutte* or maybe an unfamiliar opera by Monteverdi, they reluctantly head home.

The Glyndebourne season runs from May to August and is usually fully booked by visitors from all over the world. This operatic experience is unique; and it seems something of a miracle that it exists at all in a world where the popularization of the great opera houses has been accompanied by a notable decline in style among patrons.

Left: Operagoers at Glyndebourne, Sussex traditionally enjoy luxurious picnics in the beautiful gardens.

Overleaf: The chalk cliffs called the Seven Sisters at Cuckmere Haven are one of the famous beauty spots of the Sussex coast.

Some opera-goers make a quick pilgrimage to Glyndebourne from London or other towns in the Home Counties, but others take the opportunity to see something of the surrounding coast and downland countryside. Near the opera house is Glynde Place, a 16th-century manor house with paintings, bronzes and a working pottery. The nearest resort is Brighton, once a fishing village called Brighthelmstone, that became a centre of fashion during the Regency era. The Prince Regent commissioned the architect Nash to build the exotic Pavilion in the Victoria Gardens, near the old Steine, where the Prince kept his morganatic wife, Mrs. Fitzherbert. Much of the Regency atmosphere still persists in this leading south coast resort. Fine terraces of Georgian houses stretch east to the new Marina, which lies under the cliffs of Kemp Town. The impressive cliffs continue east, past the attractive villages of Rottingdean and Peacehaven, flattening out at the valley of the Ouse at Newhaven, then rising to a grand climax at Beachy Head.

Inland there is some fine downland country, with places of interest to visit. There is a manor house at Charleston and nearby, at Wilmington, a 70-m (231-ft) high figure of a man, dating back perhaps to the 6th century, has been cut into the chalk hills. Near Alfriston is Firle Place, the venue for an annual Wine Festival.

The Aldeburgh Music Festival takes place at the Maltings at Snape on the River Alde, at the point where it becomes navigable. The idea of creating a musical centre in the peaceful Suffolk countryside was inspired by the composer Benjamin Britten. In 1948 he founded the annual Aldeburgh Festival together with the English tenor, Peter Pears, with whom he had toured the U.S.A. and Europe as his pianist. Several of Britten's own works had their first performances at the festival. In 1967 an old complex of malt houses became the festival's permanent home. Burned

Modern sculpture decorates the grounds of the rebuilt maltings at Snape which house the concert hall and workshops created by the composer Benjamin Britten and the singer Sir Peter Pears.

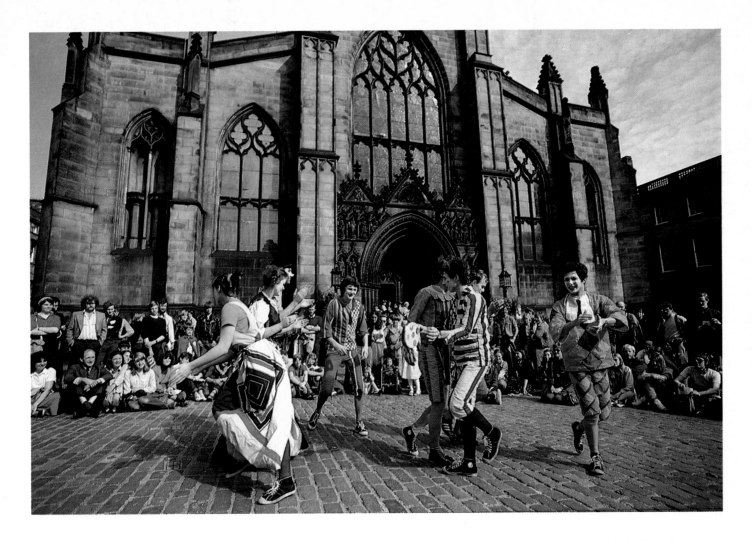

The International Edinburgh Festival held in August is enhanced by the spontaneity and colour of its fringe activities. These dancers are performing in front of St. Giles Cathedral.

down two years later, Snape Maltings was re-built and today has a concert hall, restaurants, an art gallery, a craft centre and the Britten-Pears school of Advanced Musical Studies.

Over the years, Snape Maltings concerts have extended their season, which now lasts from April to December, but the main festival season takes place in June. In August, Snape Maltings run a series of promenade concerts during which the fishing village of Aldeburgh puts on its annual Olde Marine Regatta and Carnival. The Carnival takes place in the delightful old village with its Georgian houses and its 16th-century Moot Hall by the sea. The celebrations include the choosing of a Carnival Queen, a grand and colourful procession with pipe bands and drum majorettes, athletic and swimming events, Punch and Judy shows, a charity market and a grand firework display.

Edinburgh's International Festival includes music, opera, theatre, art exhibitions, processions, street buskers and a host of fringe entertainments. There are poetry readings in pubs and there are ceilidhs, informal musical gatherings at restaurants, wine bars and cellar clubs. Festival time in Edinburgh is one of the great international cultural events and, while it lasts, the whole city is in holiday mood. And Edinburgh is a splendid setting for the Festival, with its beautiful buildings and exciting past. The city's axis lies along the Royal Mile, the long sloping street running between the castle and the Palace of Holyroodhouse. Along this historic route are Parliament House, Parliament Hall and St. Giles Cathedral. There is the house where the uncompromising Scottish reformer, John Knox, is said to have lived and Huntly House, which houses the City Observatory, the Parthenon National Monument and the Nelson Monument, from which there are fine views of the city. North of Princes Street and its shops is the New Town, built in Georgian times, with its

Above: Street theatre is another colourful and entertaining aspect of the Edinburgh Festival. Participants come from all over Britain.

elegant buildings and squares. Largely designed by James Craig, this is a tranquil residential area. However, it does contain the Music Hall – a focal point for musical activity during the Festival.

Most of the action takes place in the old town in the theatres, art galleries and concert halls on each side of the Royal Mile. Here, around the street dominated by St. Giles – the High Church of Scotland where John Knox launched the Reformation in Scotland and near which Bonnie Prince Charlie proclaimed his father King James III – is where the festival crowds have strolled to and from the shows for the 41 years since the Edinburgh Festival was founded.

Chief among the events of the festival are the theatrical performances which have a cosmopolitan character with shows and casts from such a diversity of countries as the United States, the German Democratic Republic, Japan, China, India, Ireland, Israel, France, Papua New Guinea, and many other countries.

To accommodate such a wealth of theatre every stage in Edinburgh is pressed into service, from the King's Theatre to the St. Brides Centre, the Haymarket, the Playhouse theatre and the Royal Lyceum. There are also events at the Signet Library, the Portobello Town Hall, the Assembly Hall and St. Cecilia's Hall where the famous Traverse theatre launches original plays which have often become international successes. There is also open theatre at the courtyard of the old college of the University of Edinburgh

Left: A view of Edinburgh with the castle on the left and the spire of the memorial to Sir Walter Scott rising above Princes Street gardens.

and from the Castle itself, the most popular and spectacular theatre of all, the Grand Firework display which illuminates the city's night sky.

The theatrical fare is astonishingly varied, ranging from classical drama to modern theatre and from tragedy to farce. There are magic shows, mime, dance, concerts and a jazz festival, first launched in 1978. Books have their own festival in Charlotte Square Gardens, which are bright with marquees in which a theatre and tented-German style bar are popular attractions.

Visitors to the Edinburgh Festival enjoy a bonus in the Fringe Festival, a fully fledged dynamic offspring of the main festival and only one year younger than its official parent. The Fringe has great verve and flair whether it is alternative theatre, revues, acrobatic shows or the fire eaters, jugglers and buskers that perform in the streets. There are some 1000 different Fringe events, enough to keep even the most active Festival visitor occupied, and they all add to the special atmosphere of one of Europe's most glorious cultural and fun celebrations.

The Edinburgh Festival is the high point of Scottish international festivals; in Wales the International Eisteddfod fills the same role, attracting singers and dancers from all over the world.

The International Eisteddfod of Wales grew out of the Welsh Eisteddfod tradition of competitions for singing, poetry and dancing, dating back to distant times when Celtic bards would gather together for discussion and song. By the 10th century, these bards were honoured at court and records began to appear of Pencerdd, chief of the bards, who established himself at the King's court and received a harp as a reward for his excellence. The King's bard was expected to devote his energies and talents to praising his master; and was the forerunner of Poets Laureate and Masters of the Queen's Music. As well as the chief bard, there were

The Welsh National Eisteddfod, unlike the international one at Llangollen, has changing venues but retains all its traditional rituals.

minor bards of varying degrees of talent who were adopted by baronial courts, fulfilling much the same role as the King's bard. Later, itinerant bards wandered about the countryside, entertaining audiences from all levels of society. In the 16th century, all bards were required to pass an apprenticeship under the tutelage of older bards, and to reach certain standards of excellence before being acknowledged as members of the Bardic Order. A ruling body of bards was established in the 17th century, to formulate styles and techniques and to administrate bardic festivals such as the Eisteddfods.

The ruling body of the bards, the Corsedd, still administers bardic affairs today and keeps alive the Celtic tradition which is at the heart of Welsh culture. The annual National Eisteddfod is held at a different centre every year but the International Eisteddfod is always celebrated in the town of Llangollen, in one of the loveliest vales of North Wales.

Llangollen lies on the River Dee which rises high in the Welsh mountains, at Lake Bala, and empties into the Irish Sea. At Llangollen the river flows through a deep green valley between steep wooded hills, overlooked by Castell Dinas Bran. There is a high bridge over the river, originally erected in Tudor times. This part of the river is turbulent and fast-flowing, providing an exciting course for the canoeists who compete here during the summer months. One of the most charming features of this attractive town is the house known as Plas Newydd, a timbered cottage in fine grounds, once occupied by two eccentric ladies who could count among their friends the Duke of Wellington, Wordsworth and other celebrities of the early 19th century.

The Vale of Llangollen is one of the corridors from England into Wales, between the Llantysilio and Berwyn mountains, and during festival time the quiet town of Llangollen is transformed into a busy maelstrom of

The bridge at Llangollen, built in the age of the Tudors, leads to Castle Street, a busy thoroughfare especially during the International Music Eisteddfod in July.

Above: The ruins of Castell Dinas Bran lie on the summit of a wooded hill above Llangollen from which there are superb views.

Opposite: Gloucester Cathedral, one of the venues for the Three Choirs festival, was founded as a Benedictine abbey and has a fine Norman nave. The tomb of Edward II, murdered at Berkeley Castle, lies in the choir.

colourful activity. The streets are crowded with people who flock from all over the world. There are young people wearing their national costumes – Spaniards, Yugoslavs, Greeks, Rumanians, Hungarians, Indians, Brazilians – scores of participants from every corner of the globe, coming to demonstrate that their old traditions are still very much alive.

There are competitions in singing, dancing and poetry, with prizes for a variety of categories including group, male, female and children's events. The competitions are held in a large marquee set up in a field under the imposing shadow of the hills topped by Castell Dinas Bran.

Music festivals are a feature of summertime Britain, providing a feast of entertainment for the music lover. In addition, there is the opportunity to enjoy the architecture of the buildings in which the concerts take place, and to explore the countryside around the musical venues.

One of the oldest and most unusual of these is the Three Choirs Festival, featuring the combined choirs of Gloucester, Hereford and Worcester Cathedrals. The event dates back to the 18th century, when amateur choirs performed the works of the great composer George Frederick Handel. The works of Handel were introduced in England by his patron George I, previously the Elector of Hanover. The idea of the joint choirs of three cathedrals performing Handel's choral works came about in 1715 when the concerts were organized for charitable purposes. The concerts were given in each of the three cathedral cities in turn and, in 1752, began to include secular as well as religious music. Today, the Three Choirs Festival includes music recitals and lectures in addition to the glorious choral concerts in the cathedrals.

A composer whose name is closely linked with the festival is Edward
Elgar, whose association with the Three Choirs lasted from 1911 to 1933.
Elgar, who was much inspired by the countryside around the Malvern
Hills, first conducted the choirs at Worcester Cathedral. The cathedral,
overlooking the River Severn, has foundations dating back to the 10th
century. One of the most characteristically English of cathedrals, it was
rebuilt during the 12th to 14th centuries and embodies Early English
Decorative and Perpendicular styles. The tomb of King John can be found
there, among many marvellous statues, and alongside the cathedral is the
Cloister, which connects with the remains of the old monastic buildings.

Hereford Cathedral is also by a river – the Wye, which flows from
central Wales to the Severn Estuary through some of the most beautiful
scenery in the region. Hereford is a far larger cathedral than Worcester
and, though much altered, still has the structure of the Norman church
built by Bishop Robert de Losinga and Bishop Reynelm in the 11th and
12th centuries. The tower was added in the 14th century by Bishop Adam;
and, in the 19th century, the whole building was restored. Among its
treasures, Hereford contains the supposed tomb of St. Ethelred. Ethelred
had always wanted to be buried at Hereford and, after his murder by King
Offa of Mercia, he was duly interred there. There is also a superb *Mapa
Mundi* of the 14th century and the shrine of St. Thomas Cantalupe, a
miracle-working saint, whose tomb has very fine carvings. During the
Three Choirs Festival the cathedral lawns are lively with visitors who take
the opportunity to visit the cloisters and the Bishop's Palace with its
Norman Hall. On the wall of the Bishop's Garden, in Gwynne Street,
romantics can see the plaque announcing that Nell Gwynne, mistress of
Charles II, was born in a house on the site.

Gloucester lies at the southern extremity of the triangle marked by the
three cathedral cities and has a long history stretching back to Roman
times, when it was an armed camp and river crossing. The cathedral began
its life as a Benedictine monastery. It was rebuilt in Norman times and
became a place of pilgrimage in the 14th century when it received the body
of Edward II, who was murdered at Berkeley Castle. His shrine is one of
the most interesting features of the cathedral, together with a window
made at the time of the Battle of Crécy in 1346 and a fine Lady Chapel built
in the 15th century.

The Three Choirs Festival provides one of the world's finest
opportunities to listen to choral and instrumental music in beautiful,
historic surroundings – some of it especially composed for the occasion by
such eminent composers as Elgar, Vaughan Williams, Holst, Walton, Bliss
and Britten. The festival begins with a cathedral service with choral music,
and most of the week of the festival is taken up by concerts performed in
whichever cathedral has been chosen as the centre for the year. In addition
to the great works there are organ recitals, chamber music, film
programmes and a garden party attended by performers and visitors. The
chosen city provides extra entertainments for the occasion and, in the
triangle of fine countryside between the three cathedrals, there are many
places of interest to visit – charming market towns like Ledbury, pretty
villages such as Fownhope and Much Marcle, and the spas of the Malvern
Hills.

Of all the summer music festivals in Britain, the one with the most
popular support, and on which young music lovers cut their teeth, is the
'Proms', a series of Promenade Concerts which take place in the 19th-
century Roman arena of the Albert Hall. This extraordinary building,
built in 1867, is the great London amphitheatre of music and spectacle.
During the Proms it combines both these characteristics – especially on the
last night.

The Royal Albert Hall, whose architecture was inspired by Roman arenas, is the setting for the Promenade concerts founded by Sir Henry Wood.

The idea of Promenade Concerts, where at least some of the audience could (in theory) promenade while the music was being played, was conceived by Sir Henry Wood. The concerts were launched in 1895 at the Queen's Hall, London, but the hall was destroyed by German bombers in 1941. However, by then the Proms, which Sir Henry had conducted for 46 years, had become part of the national heritage and were resumed in the Albert Hall. They have continued to be played there ever since, conducted by Sir Henry until the year before he died.

The Albert Hall's huge auditorium can seat some 5600 people, with additional standing room. The music performed at the Proms is more varied than in most series of concerts, and familiar great masters rub shoulders with such modernists as Berg, Schoenberg and Stravinsky – thus introducing a vast panorama of orchestral music to the widest audience in Britain. The last night of the Proms is a ritual occasion with a familar pattern which no one would want to change. Even before the doors of the Albert Hall open, there is a seething crowd of festively-dressed young people outside the building. Eccentric dressing and exuberant behaviour is the norm for the night. Nonetheless, when the performance begins, a well-

An audience of 8000 music lovers attend the summer Promenade concerts at the Albert Hall. This picture taken on the last night of the Proms conveys some of the atmosphere of this unique event.

The Battle of the Flowers at Jersey is renowned for the high quality of the decorated floats, many of which are later preserved in an exhibition at St. Ouen.

mannered hush falls over the hall, full of funny hats, fantastic masks and colourful robes, with balloons and banners bobbing up and down among the promenaders. But once the formal part of the concert has ended, everyone lets their hair down and the fun begins to the strains of popular songs. The grand finale is reached with the playing of Elgar's 'Land of Hope and Glory', which is lustily sung by the assembled company, with much flag waving, balloon popping and other boisterous behaviour. Simple fun but infectious, as anyone who has experienced the last night at the Proms will agree.

SUMMER BY THE SEA

A flowery celebration of high spirits in summer takes place on the Channel Islands, whose allegiance to the British monarch lies in her role as the Duke of Normandy rather than as the Queen of England. The strange political situation of the Channel Islands dates back to the time of William the Conqueror, Duke of Normandy; the islands are the last remnants of his Dukedom which have kept their allegiance intact. There are nine principal islands in the archipelago, the smallest inhabited island being Herm and the largest being Jersey. Jersey and the second largest island, Guernsey, are prosperous agricultural regions and have a flourishing tourist trade which benefits from the mild climate and beautiful coastal scenery.

Every August, Jersey celebrates the summer with a spectacular Battle of Flowers, first organized to celebrate the Coronation of Edward VII and Queen Alexandra. The procession takes place along Victoria Avenue, just as it did on the first occasion, and scores of floats adorned with flowers and depicting a variety of themes from railway engines to space craft, move down the Avenue to the music of military bands, pipe bands, steel bands and other groups of players. As well as the bands, there are several troupes of drum majorettes to delight the crowds that pack the procession route.

Left: Jersey has its own Battle of the Flowers Queen but its allegiance to the Queen of England is through her inherited title of ruler of Normandy.

Below: Charles Dickens worked on Barnaby Rudge *and* Bleak House *while staying at Broadstairs. His residence at the charming Kent resort is celebrated with a Dickens Festival.*

The growth in popularity of the Jersey Battle of Flowers has increased the number and quality of the decorated vehicles that take part. There are competitions for the best decorated cars, and prizes are awarded in a number of categories. There has also been an increased participation by Continental orchestras and representation from other flower festival resorts, such as San Remo in Italy, which have added to the international flavour of the Jersey event.

The prolific writer, Charles Dickens, who created a gallery of

Overleaf: Bournemouth in Dorset is one of the most popular English south coast resorts and a centre of cultural activity as well as bathing during summer.

173

unforgettable characters representing 19th-century English society, still contributes to the entertainment of the British and their visitors today, by inspiring two summer festivals.

The oldest of these is at Broadstairs. This festival began its life in 1937, 100 years after Dickens' first visit to this still delightful seaside resort which has retained much of its Victorian atmosphere and elegance. In June, Broadstairs becomes once again a Dickensian world, as the festival gets going with a garden party, where the guests wear Dickensian costume. At such a gathering one might run across Mr. Pickwick, Scrooge, David Copperfield, Mr. Micawber or a host of other characters from Dickens' writings. Every aspect of the festival activities conjures up Dickens; there is a Dickensian cricket match, croquet tournaments in front of the Dickens House Museum, contests of battledore and shuttlecock, a Victorian ladies bazaar, lectures at which extracts from the writer's works are read and visitors enjoy a Victorian buffet, coffee mornings and daring bathing parties in Victorian costume. The picturesque proceedings last seven days and end with a great Festival Ball at which all present turn up in their best Dickensian clothes for a splendid occasion.

The Rochester Festival was first launched nine years ago. It depicts the more rough and tumble world of Victorian England, with an accent on street life. There is a vast market that stretches the length of the High Street which is peopled with Dickensian characters and there are also Punch and Judy Shows, itinerant pedlars, rogues and press gangs looking for unwilling sailors for Her Majesty's Navy. Another Dickensian touch is the arrival of Mr. Pickwick's train from London, whose passengers pour out onto Rochester Station platform looking much as the first train travellers must have done when a day at a seaside town was still a novelty.

The Rochester Festival ends with a Grand Festival Ball. The author himself would have enjoyed this occasion, for his early days at Rochester were impecunious ones, his father being a clerk in the Navy at nearby Chatham, and he had always aspired to the gracious life. This he finally achieved due to unremitting toil and he acquired an estate at nearby Gads Hill, where he died at the tragically early age of 58.

August is a particularly festive month in Britain for it is the time when most British families take a week or two away from home, either at the seaside or in the country. The holiday mood of the entire country shows itself in the number of entertainments, competitions, fairs and sporting events that take place in towns and villages everywhere. All the seaside towns are in a celebratory mood, with their colourful and crowded beaches and the spectacle of thousands of individuals at play is a show in itself.

The climax of the month is the August Bank Holiday, which is in the last week of August (except in Scotland, which sets its own date). The holiday is regarded with mixed feelings by most people because of the conditions created by vast movements of people – the worst traffic jams of the year and crowding in every resort and centre of entertainment. However, few can resist celebrating the Bank Holiday in some way, on the beach, at inland beauty spots, cricket matches, race meetings, athletic events or at the host of other entertainments that celebrate the height of summer.

The Bank Holiday, when the whole country can be seen *en fête* is a landmark in the cycle of the seasons. Though the weather is often warm and sunny well into October, the holiday marks the end of high summer, and the return to orderly workaday rhythms of existence as the days shorten and the country takes on the golden gleam of autumn. Nevertheless, it is not the end of celebrations and ceremonies in Britain; these continue, undaunted, through the golden autumn and into the dark days of winter.

Opposite: One of the great carnival occasions of the London summer takes place at Notting Hill where a unique festival occasion is created with huge parades and fantastic costumes.

Season of Mists and Mellow Fruitfulness

In October the green tints of summer give way to a spectacular show of warm brown, gold and ochre. This scene is at Abinger Hammer, Surrey.

Autumn in the British countryside is a pageant of gentle, glowing beauty as the leaves on the trees turn to a myriad shades of yellow, brown and gold, and the grass, recovering from the summer's heat, grows lushly in the chequered fields. All over the farmlands it is harvest time. The wheat is garnered by monster machines – a far cry from the scenes of field workers bringing in the harvest painted by Constable and Gainsborough. Views over the hedgerows and trees are veiled by the smoke from burning stubble, which is watched by farmers with careful eyes. Overhead wheel great flocks of migratory birds; the swifts and swallows making their last fly-past before the long journey south. And in the hedgerows and gardens tits and robins make their busy preparations for the long winter ahead.

On Halloween a knock on the door may mean a visit by 'witches' offering a trick or treat. Refusal to grant the latter may produce a mischievous riposte.

Autumn is also a season for celebration in Britain for the weather is mild (often as warm as in the summer months), arousing in people the will to extend the summer season and keep the winter at bay. But there is another aspect to the British autumn. It is a time for reflection as well as celebration, a time when the significance of national life is brought to the public attention in such splendid and serious events as the State Opening of Parliament, Remembrance Day and, in a lighter vein, the Lord Mayor's Show.

All Saints Day on 1 November is celebrated throughout the Christian world. It is a day for the remembrance of the dead, especially close relatives, and in many countries a day of pilgrimage to cemeteries which bloom with flowers and greenery brought by the living.

The All Hallows Eve or Hallowe'en, which is the night before, 31 October, has a different connotation, and is associated with the more sinister aspects of the supernatural. It is the night when witches, goblins and other sinister creatures emerge and fear and darkness reign. The other side of the loving and caring world of All Saints Day perhaps?

In Britain, Hallowe'en has long been celebrated at gatherings where certain traditional rituals are observed. Pumpkins are hollowed out and cut to appear as grotesque faces, lit by a candle from within, apples are placed in barrels of water and picked out by participants with their teeth and candlelit processions visit graveyards. Children in outlandish witches costumes knock on doors to play 'Trick or Treat', threatening to play a, usually light-hearted, practical joke on the householder unless he gives them gifts of sweets or money. There is a generally 'spooky' atmosphere until midnight, when, according to tradition, the weirdies and ghosties fly back to whence they came and All Saints Day begins.

SPORTING AUTUMN

Nostalgia is in the air at an autumn event in Scotland – the Braemar
Highland Games. Highland Games are held throughout Scotland during
the summer, including games at Gourock, Blair Castle, Ardrossan, Skye,
Caithness, Dingwall, Drumtochty and Invergarry, and of the 70 or so such
events Braemar is the chief.

The games are rooted deep in the Scottish past when, according to
legend, Scottish chieftains would stage races up mountains to test the
stamina and character of their servants and fighting men. The tough old
clansmen were gradually softened in southern Scotland, where commerce
with England brought a gentler form of existence. Up in the Highlands,
however, cut off from the south and from each other by deep glens and
forests, the Scots remained a rugged, independent people, feuding with
each other but united against their common foe – the English and their
southern Scottish allies. It was this fierce reluctance to conform that
brought about the massacre of the Macdonalds at Glencoe, and the ill-
advised support for Bonnie Prince Charlie when he attempted to regain the
Stuart crown. After that episode the English government forbade all
Highland gatherings and the wearing of the kilt. In the 19th century,
however, old wounds were eventually healed when Queen Victoria and
Prince Albert made their summer home at Balmoral and encouraged the
holding of Highland Games at Braemar.

Since the days of Queen Victoria the Braemar gathering has continued
to grow in status and is attended by thousands of Scots, who proudly wear
their clan tartans whether taking part in the sports or merely watching.
The scene at the small village of Braemar on the River Dee is a lively one.
The stone buildings by the rushing stream are decorated with flowers and
bunting and the streets crowded with visitors who, because of their

The Royal Family, who reside at nearby Balmoral Castle during the summer, attend the Highland Games at Braemar.

number, can only enter the games area by ticket. Around the village, hills rise in all directions – to the south their lower slopes are covered with the Ballochbuie forest, planted by Queen Victoria, and to the north Cullardoch rises to over 878 m (2900 ft). The village of Braemar was once a rallying point for the Earl of Mar, who built a castle there in 1715, during the Jacobite Rebellion in support of the Old Pretender, Bonnie Prince Charlie's father. Later, another castle, the ruins of which still stand, was built by the River Dee.

Balmoral Castle is some 6 miles down river and its grounds are open to the public when the Royal Family is not in residence. Nearby is little Crathie Church where the Royal Family attend services during their visits to Balmoral. Further down the Dee are Aboyne, Crathes and Drum Castles and in the hills to the north is the tower-like Craigevar Castle, with its turrets and pinnacles. Not far away is 17th-century Leith Hall. The Dee rises in the Grampian mountains and enters the sea at Aberdeen. It is not difficult to see why Queen Victoria called the region along its course her 'dear Paradise' for it possesses some of Scotland's finest scenery.

The Braemar Games include many events that have become standard in the world of athletics. However, two of the events are traditionally and uniquely Scottish. The Throwing of the Weight is a test said to have originated in the soldierly sport of pitching heavy cannon balls in friendly competitions. The Tossing of the Caber is the other Scottish event. The caber is a tree trunk which athletes must carry upright for a few yards before tossing it in the air to fall as far as possible and as straight as possible ahead of them. Cabers vary in size, but the Braemar Caber is said to be the most formidable, weighing 54.5 kgs (120 lbs) and measuring 5.79 m (19 ft) in length. The present caber dates from 1951 when it was first tossed by 51-year-old George Clarke, a famous caber champion.

The caber, a tall tree-trunk, is tossed by Scottish athletes who need the skill to balance it as well as the strength to project it.

Blair Castle, the venue for the World Piping Championship, is a beautiful and historic building visited by Edward III and Mary Queen of Scots, stormed by Cromwell and held by the Duke of Cumberland before Culloden.

The animation of the Highland Games ground with its marquees and stalls is heightened by various other activities that take place, such as Highland dancing and bagpipe performances. Even without these additional attractions, the colour and conviviality of this truly Scottish occasion are unique and attract thousands of visitors from Britain and overseas year after year.

Good lungs and stamina are also needed to play the bagpipes. The World Piping Championships are held in October and attract entries from Scots who have settled all over the world, as well as those who have stayed in their native land.

The venue for this stirring competition is Blair Castle at Blair Atholl in Perthshire, a beautiful part of the Scottish Highlands near the Pass of Killiecrankie. It was here that Graham of Claverhouse, 'Bonnie Dundee', defeated the English during the Convenanter War of the 17th century when the Scots fought to defend their Presbyterian faith.

Today, Killiecrankie is a lovely and tranquil place where the River Garry tumbles through a steep wooded gorge towards its junction with the River Tummel which flows from the enchanting lochs of Tummel and Rannoch.

Blair Atholl lies to the north of Killiecrankie, with the castle situated alongside the charming village in its wooded parkland. The oldest part of the castle is the Cumming's Tower of 1269 and much of the rest goes back to the 16th century. The castle contains a fine collection of portraits, an armoury and a natural history museum. The Piping Championships are held in the Great Hall, a splendid beamed room decorated with swords, halberds, tabards and other warlike equipment of former times. The competition is held before an audience, and judges adjudicate as the

The art of piping reaches a climax every year at Blair Castle when Scottish pipers show off their musical ability at the World Championship.

stirring music rings out, evoking Scotland's romantic past and the battles where the pipes spurred on the warriors.

A rather more intense affair is the annual marathon up the slopes of Ben Nevis, run in September. This is as much a ritual as a race, for Britain's highest mountain is a legendary place – a kind of Scottish Mount Olympus – and the climbing of it a form of homage.

The race begins at Fort William, built by General Monk to keep the Highlanders in order in the 17th century. The town has one long main street which runs parallel to Loch Linnhe and lies to the west of Ben Nevis. The surrounding countryside is very attractive. To the north-west of the town lies the Great Glen, which cuts through the Highlands to Inverness and was once a useful waterway, its lochs, rivers and canals linking the North and Irish Seas. With the development of rail and road transport, the canal was used less and less and today it serves as a waterway for pleasure craft, which can sail from loch to loch through the system. To the south-west, Loch Linnhe flows past Loch Leven and the spectacular valley of Glencoe, towards the Isle of Mull and the town of Oban. To the west lies the Road to the Isles which leads to Skye, the embarkation point for the Outer Hebrides.

The Ben Nevis runners follow the path up the west slopes of the mountain. Visitors can usually walk to the summit in about four hours, but the runners manage to race to the summit and back in an hour and a half. The spectators take up their positions along the course: some line the lower slopes, looking up the valley towards the mountain, while others climb up to the plateau which is traversed by a zig-zag path as it approaches the summit. A ruined observatory sits at the top. The view from the summit is spectacular and, on a clear day, extends over some 100

There is no lack of enthusiasm among competitors who toil up the slopes of Ben Nevis above Fort William. Here they are halfway up and running strongly.

Spectators who have climbed Ben Nevis earlier in the day wait to cheer the runners as they reach the summit.

Racers set off from Llanberis for the gruelling Snowdonia Marathon in North Wales.

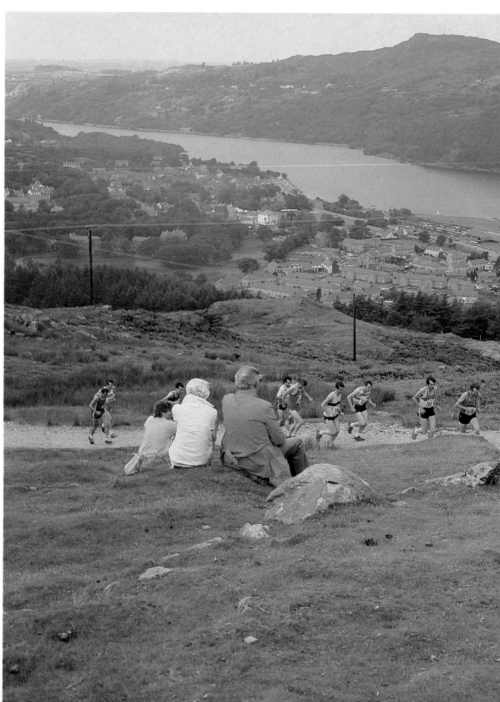

miles – to the Grampian mountains to the east and the Hebrides to the west. The runners are usually too busy to enjoy the view, but spectators can do so and, if they have time, walk up Glen Nevis with its steep rugged valley. In the evening, after the race, there is music and song in the hostelries of Fort William, and many tales of the exploits of the runners.

The second highest mountain in Britain, Snowdon in Wales, also has a ritual marathon in the autumn, attracting no less than 700 runners. In addition, thousands of spectators come to watch the race and pay their own tribute to the mountain which the Welsh call Y Wyddfa Fawr – the great tomb of the giant Fawr, who was slain by King Arthur.

The rendezvous for racers and spectators for the great Snowdonia Marathon is Llanberis. This village lies between lakes Padarn and Peris. It is the terminus for the Snowdonia railway and the start of the Llanberis track, one of the six traditional paths to the summit.

The starting point for the marathon lies to the south of Lake Peris, at the foot of the formidable Llanberis Pass at Nant Peris (Old Llanberis). The runners race up the pass, with its steep wall and screes, to Pen-Y-Pass at the summit of the pass, the starting point for two other routes up Snowdon. The runners then follow the road downhill past lakes Gwynant

and Dinas, which lie at the foot of Snowdon lending a magnificent background to the wooded valley. At the bottom of the valley is Beddgelert, where large crowds await the racers who have almost reached the half-way mark.

The village of Beddgelert is delightful, with stone houses set among trees under the lee of steep overhanging cliffs. Once the site of a monastery and a port, linked to the sea by the Glaslyn river which still runs busily through the village, Beddgelert is now a favourite holiday destination. Visitors are attracted by its scenery and walks and also by the shrine of the legendary hound, Gelert, owned by King Llewellyn. According to the legend, Llewellyn left Gelert in charge of his young son. On returning to find his

The mountains of North Wales provide spectacular scenery for walkers and lovers of the open air. This view is of Cader Idris looking south from Cernian in Gwynedd.

son gone and the hound covered in blood, he jumped to the wrong conclusion and killed the dog. He soon discovered that his son was unharmed and a large wolf had been slain by the faithful Gelert. Aghast at his mistake, the King buried his hound, with full honours.

The racers pass swiftly through the village and up the valley of Beddgelert Forest to Pont Cae Gors, at 181 m (600 ft), before descending to Lake Cwellyn. They race on to Waunfawr for the final 5 miles of the marathon, first up the steep hill to Bwlch'-Y-Goes and then the final downhill run to Llanberis.

The marathon is an event that draws thousands of visitors to Snowdonia in November, a month when the weather can be dry and even sunny though the daylight hours are shortening. The valleys, with their autumn colourings, and the purple and blue summits of the mountains make a fine contrast and many people take the opportunity presented by a visit to the marathon to spend a day or two touring Snowdonia before the winter sets in. All around the Snowdonia National Park there are natural wonders galore. To the south lies another giant among mountains, Cader Idris, and to the east the Lleyn peninsula stretches a protective arm over Cardigan Bay. To the north is the island of Anglesey, separated from the mainland by the historic Menai Strait. Edward I built his famous castle at Caernarvon, at the south-western end of Anglesey, and also created the title of Prince of Wales for Royal heirs. At the north-eastern end of the island he built Beaumaris, the last of his Welsh castles and one of the most interesting, with its sea-filled moat and projecting bastions. In 1819 the road bridge joining mainland Wales to Anglesey was built by the engineer Thomas Telford and in 1850 the railway bridge was built.

North of Snowdonia lie the Welsh seaside resorts of Llandudno and Colwyn Bay and, at the mouth of the Conwy river, another castle rises above the attractive little town of Conwy. The Vale of Conwy, which runs from Conwy to Betws-y-Coed, is one of the most beautiful in Wales with green wooded slopes and pretty villages. At Betws-y-Coed, roads from Bangor, Caernarvon and the southern part of Wales meet. This lovely village is a popular and convenient stopping place for visitors.

One of the great houses of Lincolnshire, Burghley House, south of Stamford, is the venue for the Burghley Horse Trials, a great equestrian autumn event. The manor of Stamford was inherited by Elizabeth I's most important adviser, William Cecil, later Lord Burghley, in 1552. In 1553 he began building a splendid new house on his land. Today, still owned and occupied by a Cecil, the Marquess of Exeter, Burghley House stands as one of the largest and grandest houses surviving from the age of the first Elizabeth.

Inside the house there are 18 treasure-filled state rooms, including the Heaven Room, the finest painted room in England. Outside there is a glorious deer park, landscaped by 'Capability' Brown and home to a handsome herd of deer. It is in this deer park that the famous Burghley Horse Trials are held every year early in September.

A three-day event was first held at Burghley in 1961 and today the Burghley Horse Trials rival in importance the trials at Badminton. On four occasions the European Three-Day Event Championship has been decided at Burghley and on two the World Championship. The European Young Riders Championship has also been held once at Burghley. Princess Anne and her former polo pony, Doublet, won the European Championship at Burghley in 1971.

Although it is a 'three-day' event, the Burghley Horse Trials are actually held over four days. On the first two days the competitors perform their dressage tests. The third day is the really exciting day for both competitors and spectators. This is the testing speed and endurance phase, when

Overleaf: A quiet moment exercising for the Burghley Horse Trials which take place in the grounds of Burghley House, Lincolnshire, a superb Elizabethan mansion.

Right: Skill and courage are needed in the cross-country phase of the trials at Burghley.

Opposite: Visitors to the English vineyards at Alfriston, Sussex in September gather at Drusilla's Corner for some wine tasting.

competitors must complete a long roads and tracks course and follow it up with the gruelling cross-country phase. The huge and difficult fences and obstacles require all the skill and courage the riders and their horses can summon up. The fourth day is the show jumping phase; since just a pole off a jump, a hoof in the water or a brick out of a wall can cost horse and rider the big prize, this is also a tense and exciting day.

More than 150,000 people visit Burghley during the trials. Each year they will see around 100 horses from many countries competing, ridden by most of the big names in the sport. When not watching the horses, they can go shopping, for Burghley always has a big shopping area where, on some 200 stands, just about everything the horse-loving, horse-owning person might need can be purchased. There are stands selling saddlery and tack, books, 'horsey' bric-a-brac or the most fashionable country clothing and footwear. There are even stands offering the opportunity to have your horse painted or photographed.

LAST OF THE SUMMER WINE

A new autumn festival in the British calendar is one celebrating the wine harvest. Although the Romans planted vineyards in Britain, and the Normans also practised viticulture, the business of grape growing and wine-making has been neglected in Britain for hundreds of years. Thirty years ago an enterprising group, headed by Sir Guy Salisbury Jones,

decided to revive the English wine industry and planted a vineyard at Hambledon in Hampshire – the same village that gave birth to the game of cricket. During the next few years, their example was followed by many others and there are now some 200 growers in Britain, some as far north as Studley Manor near Stratford-upon-Avon and Lexham Hall in Norfolk.

In 1975 the English vineyards held their first Wine Festival at Michelham Priory and, in 1981, the event moved to a permanent site at the English Wine Centre at Alfriston, Sussex. Since then, the festival has been an increasing success, with over 4000 visitors to the 2-day event at which some 30 vineyards exhibit their products and offer wine tastings. As well as the wines of English vineyards such as Lamberhurst, Carr Taylor, Barton Manor, Rock Lodge, etc., there is a wide selection of regional English foods on offer, to complement the wines.

The festival is a leisurely affair, as visitors move from stand to stand tasting wines, or relax on grassy slopes listening to a jazz band or watching roving entertainers. There is also a grape-treading competition, for those who feel energetic.

A Cumbrian celebration of harvest time is the Egremont Crab Fair, the crab referring to apples, not crustaceans. The fair takes place at Egremont, near Whitehaven, and probably dates back to the 13th century. At midday there is a sudden bustle in the High Street and a cart (nowadays it is more likely to be a lorry), piled high with apples makes its appearance. All the spectators line the pavements as soon as it appears, for they know that what comes next is a free distribution of apples which are thrown from the apple-laden vehicle as it trundles its way down the street.

This is only one of the traditional events which make Egremont Fair different to other fairs. In the middle of the High Street is a greasy pole liberally covered with soap and other slimy substances and at the top of the pole is a prize. The challenge is evident; who can reach the top of the pole and grab the prize? Competitors resort to all kind of techniques to get to the top, even climbing on each other's shoulders. The competition provides fun for onlookers and participants and is a high spot of the day's activities, which include track and field contests, hound trials in the Cumbrian style, Westmoreland wrestling, and a dog show.

In the evening there is a funny joke competition, fast pipe smoking contests and a Gurning Championship. 'Gurning' means pulling a hideous face, and there are plenty of entrants for this gruesome contest, at which the crabbiest face wins.

One of the oldest autumn fairs in Britain is the Mop Fair at Tewkesbury, which was granted a charter by Elizabeth I. Like other Mop Fairs the

Opposite: Climbing the greasy pole at the Egremont Crab Fair is no easy task though it helps when there are other shoulders to stand on.

Left: The old market town of Tewkesbury on the Warwickshire Avon is the site of a famous country fair where old crafts are demonstrated.

London's Pearly Kings and Queens clad in their pearl button clothes celebrate the Costermongers' Harvest Festival at the church of St. Martin-in-the-Fields at Trafalgar Square.

Tewkesbury one was a hiring fair, where farmers went to look for labourers to work the land for them and householders hired domestic help. Sometimes children of poor families would be taken off to work in the big house and rarely saw much of their home again.

Today the Tewkesbury Fair is more of a pleasure fair with all the modern fairground attractions which bring the public from miles around.

IN THE COUNTRYSIDE

In the countryside, autumn is harvest time. The last of the grain is gathered, the hay is stored in barns and the root crops are collected. Tractors plough up the fields, followed by crowds of sea gulls hovering and diving over the open furrows as the earth is turned. Village halls are decorated with flowers and fruit and children set to work making corn dollys to sell at the Harvest Festivals.

One of the oldest of the autumn festivals still in existence is the Nottingham Goose Fair, whose charter, granted by Edward I in 1284, gave Royal sanction to a fair that had actually been being held long before that. The Fair is thought to have been started by the Danes, who had a settlement in Nottingham. Originally, the Fair was a market, enabling people to buy and sell their produce before the onset of winter. How the fair acquired the name 'Goose' Fair is not known for certain. However, geese were a part of the basic diet of medieval people, and the flat lands stretching eastward were good breeding grounds for these birds, which would be driven to market in large flocks rather like sheep. The history of the Goose Fair, like that of most traditional fairs, is also a story of the social changes that have taken place in Britain since medieval times. In those days fairs were market places for the sale of local produce, operated under licence of the King or Lord of the Manor. Usually fairs took place in

There may not be any geese at Nottingham Goose Fair today but there is every fairground entertainment imaginable.

spring and autumn, their function being to provide produce for a whole season to a populace that had little mobility beyond places they could reach on foot. This function of a fair continued until the end of the 18th century, when the Industrial Revolution changed the life of the British population in the course of one or two generations.

As Nottingham's industries increased, its population grew and country people began to pour into the factories that offered work. Obviously, the increase in population created a greater demand for market produce but, with the greater mobility provided by the railways, it ceased to be necessary to store sacks of potatoes, strings or onions, scores of cheeses or bushels of apples to see a household through a winter season. Instead, this produce became instantly available at retail shops which arose to serve the new clientèle. To provide the shops with farm produce a new entrepreneur group of wholesalers evolved, buying goods from the farmer in order to re-sell them to the shops which, in turn, sold them to the public. This new way of doing business struck an almost mortal blow to the Nottingham Goose Fair, a blow which was aggravated by the removal of the cattle-trading section to another site, followed by the setting up of a wholesale market elsewhere.

Having lost the *raison d'être* that had kept it going since its foundation, the fair almost closed down but, with the invention of steam-powered engines, it took on a new lease of life as a funfair. Ornate roundabouts with brightly coloured horses and a steam organ, huge powered swings that looked like stage coaches, trains as elaborate as the Lord Mayor's coach were added to such traditional fairground attractions as the boxing booth and donkey rides.

For the army of factory workers the new fair provided colour and excitement in their otherwise drab, workaday lives and soon the Nottingham Goose Fair was a roaring success again, with visitors arriving from all over the Midlands for the week-long jamboree. Unfortunately, the fair also became an arena for the release of pent-up feelings of frustration at the sordid conditions of life for the workers; and drunkenness and violence brought the fair under threat once again. Happily, with the improvement of working conditions and improved surveillance of unruly elements, the rowdy atmosphere was dissipated, and the fair, which in 1928 moved from the Market Place in the centre of

The largest fair in Britain was first granted a charter in 1284 by Edward I. Today the Nottingham Goose Fair is officially opened each year at the beginning of October.

These fine 'gallopers' make their annual appearance at the fair and are a reminder of the fine craftsmanship of the age before mass production.

Overleaf: Skittling is a popular event at West Country fairs such as this one at Widecombe-in-the-Moor.

The village of Widecombe-in-the-Moor is beautifully situated on the eastern edges of Dartmoor. Its 14th–16th century church, with its 36.6-m (120-ft) tower, is known as the 'Cathedral of Dartmoor'.

town into the Forest Recreation Ground, became the popular autumn attraction that it is today.

The new Nottingham Goose Fair is still a great gathering place for people from all the towns and villages around Nottingham. Nowadays it possesses all the most sophisticated fairground rides, as well as stalls where you can try your luck at winning a stuffed toy, goldfish or some other fairground souvenir. Among the 400 stalls there are those that keep up the old market traditions and sell everything from carpets to candy floss, and food stalls selling solid Nottingham fare of sausages and mushy peas or Grantham gingerbread, just as they did a hundred years ago.

Nottinghamshire was of course Robin Hood's county and memories of the outlaw of Sherwood Forest still remain. In the city you will find the site of the castle lived in by Robin's enemy, the Sheriff of Nottingham, though the building on the 40 m (133 ft) crag was rebuilt in the 19th century and now houses the Museum and Art Gallery. Sherwood forest stretches north – though little now remains of its densely wooded areas. However, there are several important houses to visit in the vicinity. Newstead Abbey, once the home of Lord Byron, lies to the north-west. The Abbey, which was originally built by Henry II to atone for the murder of Thomas à Becket, now contains many Byronic mementoes, including the table on which he wrote some of Childe Harolde. Hardwick Hall, one of the finest Elizabethan houses in England, lies to the north, beyond the town of Mansfield. The house belonged to the formidable Bess of Hardwick, an Elizabethan lady of strong character and considerable influence. The hall has exceptionally large and beautiful windows and a gallery with a

painting of Mary Queen of Scots, whose jailer was Sir William Cavendish, Bess of Hardwick's husband. Another grand house is 19th-century Thoresby Hall, in the northern extremity of Sherwood Forest, and here there are traces of the Robin Hood legend and a statue of Robin in the grounds. Nearby, at Edwinstone, is the church of St. Mary where Robin married Maid Marian.

In the glorious setting of the West Country two other great autumn fairs take place, both maintaining a truly rural character, founded on the local farming communities round about.

The first of the traditional West Country autumn fairs takes place in Widecombe-in-the-Moor. This tiny grey stone village, with its church tower rising up like a lighthouse, is surrounded by wild moorland, offering splendid views on clear days. However, in autumn and winter, it is often wrapped in the thick mists so vividly described by Conan Doyle in *The Hound of the Baskervilles* – a story set in Manaton, a few miles to the north-east. The fair has been immortalized in the song which recounts how Tom Cobbleigh and his friends, Bill Brewer, Jan Stewer, Peter Gurney, Dan'l Whiddon, Harry Hawk and all, went riding on Tom Pearse's grey mare and were carried off into the mists, never to be seen again.

Today Widecombe Fair is still in existence and attracts huge crowds to this magical moorland spot. The centre of activities is the tiny village square, where there is a good pub and an attractive National Trust shop next to the church. On the day of the fair the lanes leading off the square are lined with stalls selling all kinds of produce. The crowds stop to listen

From Dartmoor there are superb views towards Tavistock and Bodmin Moor in Cornwall.

to the Master of Ceremonies, who announces the events of the day dressed in a shepherd's smock to commemorate the fair's origins as a sheep market. Outside the pub morris dancers leap, the ribbons at their knees and elbows fluttering to the agile movements of the dance. Accordion and guitar players stroll among the crowds. Traditional games are played in a nearby field; strong youths grapple with the greasy pole, while others set off on a cross-country run. There are pony races and obstacle races to keep the crowds entertained; and a lunch-time meal of Devon pasties and cider to keep their energy up.

The Tavistock Goose Fair dates back to the 12th century, when Henry I granted a charter for the fair to a Benedictine Abbey. Little of the original Abbey can now be seen among the Victorian rebuilding, but the gatehouse tower and cloisters remain. Tavistock became rich as one of the stannary towns where tin, mined locally, was weighed and stamped; and the Fair, under the direction of the Abbey, grew in size until the Dissolution of the Monasteries by Henry VIII restricted the Abbey's participation.

Later the 'Goozey Fair', as it is popularly known, was revived and has continued up to the present day in the town's Bedford Square. The fair starts at 6 a.m., when the stallholders arrive and the impressive 19th-century roundabout, with its brightly coloured baroque horses and brass fittings, begins to turn slowly to the sound of its organ pipes. It is soon joined by other fairground attractions, with themes spanning the years from horse-drawn transport to the space age. As the crowds arrive the stallholders cry out their tempting offers: 'Three rings for 50p', 'Have a go! Win a goldfish or a bottle of ginger wine', 'Here you are, win a lovely coconut', and so on. Meanwhile, the air is filled with the smell of frying onions and sizzling hamburgers, together with the sweet scent of candy floss. Between rides, the visitors stroll round the market stalls, examining the shelves of old books, the blankets and bed linen, the potted plants, china ornaments and all the other exotic bric-à-brac of a country fair.

Nearby, outside the town centre, the livestock fair is also in progress. Cattle stand patiently in pens or are herded to the dealers' tent, where the

Built in the 13th century by Cistercian monks, Buckland Abbey was converted in 1576 into a country house. Sir Francis Drake bought it and lived there until his death in 1596. The nearby village keeps its medieval name of Buckland Monachorum ('of the monks').

auctioneer calls out the bids and finalizes a transaction with a tap of his hammer. There are sheep, ponies and chickens too, as well as some geese – far fewer than in the days when they gave their name to the fair. Many of the geese end up on the tables of local restaurants, which lay on special menus for the Goose Fair. The celebrations go on all day and late into the night, with much revelry in the local pubs, where barrels of 'scrumpy' (cider) provide the authentic refreshment for this Devon festival.

For visitors to the fair who take the opportunity to stay a while in the area, there are plenty of interesting things to do and see. To the south lies medieval Cotehele House, containing fine tapestries and furniture. There is Buckland Abbey, founded in 1278, which became the home of Sir Francis Drake. The tithe barn and church tower from the original building have been incorporated in the present house, which is a Drake and West

As part of the annual Taunton Carnival, a barrel race takes place through the streets of the town to celebrate the harvesting of the cider apples. Competitors have to wear either the 'traditional' Somerset smock or carnival dress.

Country Museum. Nearby is the village of Buckland Monachorum and its lovely garden. To the north of Tavistock, on the road to Okehampton, is the pretty village of Lydford with its ruined castle, once a prison for stannary offenders, and its deep gorge which can be explored on foot. To the east of Tavistock across the loneliest part of Dartmoor, past Two Bridges where the moor roads intersect, is Princeton, where the notorious Dartmoor prison, so often featured in Victorian thrillers, is situated.

Widecombe Fair recalls the days when the wool trade was England's main source of foreign revenue. Another, better-known West Country

Old-world Somerset 'babes' add to the atmosphere of the Taunton Carnival and its colourful parade of illuminated floats.

trade is commemorated in the town of Taunton – that is the apple-growing and cider-making industry which has long been associated with Somerset and Devon.

The busy country town of Taunton was once the scene of Judge Jeffreys' Bloody Assize, which brought to harsh justice supporters of the Duke of Monmouth, Charles II's illegitimate son, who had tried to seize the throne from his uncle, James II. Taunton's features of interest include a castle, originally built in the 12th century and now used as a museum, and a fine perpendicular-style church. Some of the town's streets are very old and these are thronged at the time of the Taunton Barrel Rolling Race and Carnival. The race is the preliminary to the Carnival procession and is run over a half-mile uphill course, with participants dressed in period costume or fancy dress. The origin of the race is not precisely known, but it probably arose from the ceremonies held at the time of the apple harvest. The barrel is rolled down the streets, swaying from side to side, producing excitement and amusement for the spectators. There follows a $1\frac{1}{2}$ mile procession of brightly lit floats, as much as 24 m (80 ft) long, decorated as pirate ships, castles etc., or with tableaux of life in days gone by. Bands, itinerant musicians and other entertainers follow the procession and stroll about the crowded town late into the night, adding to the colour and character of this typical West Country festival.

CRINOLINES AND MOTORIZED CARRIAGES

A celebration with its roots in more recent history takes place at Llandrindod Wells, in Wales. Once a famous spa, the town was not only famous for its chalybeate- and sulphur-laden waters, but also for the gambling clubs, dancing rooms and other racy establishments that existed to entertain the gentlemen who arrived to take the waters.

It would be easy to think the clock has been turned back one hundred years at Llandrindod's Victorian Festival, for all the townspeople join in the festival atmosphere.

Llandrindod Wells is the perfect setting for its ten-day Victorian festival. The architecture of the late 19th century, when the spa was built, has been preserved almost completely intact. Wide avenues bordered by imposing brick buildings, with well laid out gardens and parks, are characteristic of this town in central Wales. In the Rock Park is the Pump Room, where taking the waters was also an excuse for social intercourse. The Pump Room is surrounded by secluded walks, leading to the River Eithon and the bowling green, which must have been ideal for the discreet flirtations that the Victorians practised.

Much of the atmosphere of the Victorian era is preserved at the Llandrindod Festival. Motor vehicles are kept out of the town centre, and are replaced by horse drawn gigs and phaetons filled with costumed passengers. All the inhabitants of the town wear Victorian costume, as do many of the visitors. Shops are managed by frock-coated gentlemen, assisted by ladies in aprons and starched caps. In the restaurants all the waiters wear stiff white shirts and black trousers, with impeccable white cloths protecting them from spillage from their waists to their knees. The streets are full of Victorian characters. The sweep in his top hat cycles by with his sooty brushes; the postman, the road sweeper, the Dickensian urchin, the street entertainers and conjurers all conspire to turn back the clock at this unique festival.

The ten days of the Festival are filled with events to complement the theme. There are Victorian melodramas at the Albert Hall Theatre, concerts at the Grand Pavilion, comedians and can-can dancers, lantern slide shows, exhibitions of fashions in petticoats, stays and dresses, veteran cycle races, *thé dansants*, Punch and Judy shows and a grand carnival procession and firework display.

In addition to all this, there is a good deal to interest the visitor in the

surrounding countryside. Castell Collen lies nearby, the site of a Roman fort. To the south is Builth Wells, another spa, set in the splendid valley of the Wye. The River Wye flows south, then east, entering England just north of the town of Hay-on-Wye which, over the years, has grown into a centre for the antiquarian book trade, where you will find scores of second-hand bookshops. South of the Wye, and within some 15 miles of Llandrindod Wells, are the Black Mountains and Brecon Beacons – areas of spectacular scenic beauty on the northern edge of the Welsh coal valleys. To the north of Llandrindod Wells is a particularly wild and attractive region of the Cambrian mountains with very little habitation. Near Rhayader, some 10 miles from Llandrindod Wells, are some fine artificial lakes. Because of its central position in Wales, Llandrindod Wells is an excellent centre for exploring the lovely Welsh countryside. Open-air activities such as pony trekking, walking and fishing are the attractions for holiday visitors.

Another nostalgic celebration is the Veteran Car Run from London to Brighton, which looks back to the last years of Victoria's reign and the early part of the Edwardian period. Wrapped up in cloaks and overcoats against the nip in the autumn air, gentlemen in deerstalkers and ladies in hats held firmly to their heads with chiffon scarves gather in Hyde Park ready for the historic drive. Lined up under the trees, on a carpet of brown and gold autumn leaves, there are vehicles carrying such aristocratic and evocative names as Daimler, Renault, Peugeot, Serpollet, Dion Bouton, Panhard, Benz and Mercedes. The brass on the cars that pioneered motor transport shines proudly in the morning sun and engines sputter into life, giving off little puffs of blue smoke from their exhausts. The crowds of spectators, many of whom have breakfasted early at the nearby Park Lane hotels, gaze at the veteran vehicles as if they were works of art.

Wales is ideal for pony trekking. This trio of riders are enjoying the open countryside of the Brecon Beacons National Park.

209

There is no undignified rush at the start; the cars set off sedately on their way south to Brighton and the south coast. The early morning traffic is beginning to move and the smooth modern cars look like metallic clones when compared to the rugged individualism of their forebears. The veterans cross Westminster Bridge, under the shadow of Big Ben, threading their way through the Borough of Lambeth down to Streatham and then Croydon. Once past Purley and Coulsdon the veterans break out into the countryside, engines chugging gamely – though an occasional stop has to be made for adjustments, or a drop of water in the radiator. Over the North Downs progress is slow, but the cars press on, guarded by their modern descendants who travel in support. They carry on down into the Weald of Kent, through Redhill and Horley, the noise of their engines sometimes drowned by aircraft headed for Gatwick airport. There is the last struggle to the South Downs and, finally, the veterans arrive panting at the Brighton seafront, passing the exotic Pavilion and slowing down as they approach the Palace Pier. They draw up on Madeira Drive where they receive the accolade of the crowds for their fine performance.

In the evening, after the cars have been lovingly locked away in garages, there is much festivity in Brighton. The competitors join in the Grand Ball,

A magnificent vintage vehicle with all its brass gleaming rolls triumphantly along in the Veteran Car Run from London to Brighton.

where awards are presented and speeches made. The enthusiasts who have followed them dine at the restaurants in the Lanes. Once the old village of Brighthelmstone, the Lanes form a delightful enclave of small restaurants and bistros, antique shops, boutiques and other establishments that please the eye and tempt the pocket.

PAGEANTRY AND PLOTS

The State Opening of Parliament after the summer recess is one of those noble occasions when the true significance and achievements of British political life are highlighted with due pomp and ceremony. This archaic ceremony, with participants dressed in costumes that date back to medieval times, serves as a dignified reminder of the system of parliamentary government which Britain has evolved over at least 800 years of the country's existence.

The growth of parliamentary government dates back to the time of William the Conqueror. It was he who adapted the existing Saxon councils of the then loosely integrated country into consultative meetings of the Barons he had appointed throughout the land. The name Parliament, from the French *parler* (to talk), was given to these councils, through which both the Barons and the Church wielded considerable power. Following the introduction of the parliamentary system, the Barons and the Church gradually curtailed the power of the King, the Barons through the Magna Carta of 1215 and the baronial revolt and the Church through its immense power as a moral force and because it administered large estates from which the King derived revenue. A third class of people whose influence in Parliament grew were the merchants, especially the rich wool merchants, whose valuable contribution to the country's economy is symbolized today by the Woolsack on which the Lord Chancellor still sits.

Neither Barons nor Church, however, were able to survive the growth of monarchical power which culminated in the accession of Henry VII after the Wars of the Roses. During the Tudor period the monarchy was supreme; strong enough to subdue the Barons and to destroy the power of the Church when Henry VIII split with Rome and dissolved the monastic system. Growing unrest during the Stuart period and the eventual execution of Charles I brought an end to the idea of an all-powerful ruler for ever. Since then, Parliament has gradually evolved as a system of government whereby the widest interests of all sections of the people are

The splendid Irish State Coach carries the Queen to the Palace of Westminster for the State Opening of Parliament after the summer recess. In exceptional circumstances Parliament may be dissolved and re-elected in mid-term. The official opening of the new Parliament then follows irrespective of the time of year.

represented by their freely elected members of Parliament. The role of the monarchy has continued as a constitutional one; the Queen does have the power to call for the formation of a government and she exerts an intangible, but nonetheless very real, moral influence on the nation.

The ceremonial of the Opening of Parliament, therefore, is not just colourful pageantry, but an affirmation of a system of government which has been long, and sometimes painful, in the making. The ceremony begins with a strange ritual in which the cellars of the Houses of Parliament are searched in remembrance of the day in November 1605 when Guy Fawkes and his fellow conspirators attempted to blow up Parliament and destroy its hard-won freedom. Unhappily, today, the search is not just a token acknowledgment of a failed coup in the past; it is part of a wider search that is constantly performed, intensified on special occasions, against modern terrorist perils.

On the day chosen for the State Opening, usually in October or November, the Queen drives in the Irish State Coach from Buckingham Palace to the Houses of Parliament. Crowds gather in the square before the Palace to see the Queen leave and line the Mall to watch the procession, standing in front of the walls of St. James's Palace, Clarence House and Marlborough House. The scene is as impressive and heart-stirring as any royal progress. The Household Cavalry, with their waving plumes and shining armour take part, and Guardsmen line the route. Included in the procession is the carriage which carries the Royal Regalia – the Imperial State Crown, the Cap of Maintenance (which signifies the monarch's duty to preserve religious orthodoxy) and the Sword of State, symbol of justice.

At Admiralty Arch the procession enters Trafalgar Square and turns down Whitehall, past the Admiralty, the Horse Guards, the Inigo Jones Banqueting House (all that remains of Whitehall Palace), the Treasury, the simple monolith of the Cenotaph and Downing Street, finally arriving in Parliament Square. A military band plays and the Queen is met by a welcoming committee headed by the Earl Marshal of England and the Lord Great Chamberlain, who is Keeper of the Royal Palace of Westminster (more usually known as the Houses of Parliament). The Queen enters the House of Lords with Prince Philip, accompanied by a procession of the highest in the land dressed in their traditional robes. When the Queen is seated on the throne, the Lord Chancellor approaches and presents her with the speech in which she will reveal the plans of her government for the following year.

There now follows a strange little drama – a reminder of the historical evolution of parliamentary rule. The members of the House of Commons are summoned to the House of Lords to hear the speech. This ritual appears to confirm the authority of the Lords over the Commons, but it is in fact a confirmation of the power of the Commons. Since the time of Charles I, who violated the privileges of the Commons, reigning monarchs have not been allowed inside the House of Commons and therefore have to request that the Commons visit them in the House of Lords. This is done by sending Black Rod as messenger. He is at first refused entry, then the Commons relent and follow their Speaker into the Lords.

This ritual having been observed, the reading of the Queen's Speech takes place and the ceremony, to which only a few members of the public are admitted, follows its course until the final words from the Queen, 'I pray that the blessings of Almighty God may rest upon your counsels', are spoken. The Queen then returns to her carriage and the procession makes its way back to Buckingham Palace, amid the cheers of the waiting crowds.

Guy Fawkes, whose treachery originally caused the instigation of the ritual search before the Opening of Parliament is remembered in a different manner. On November the fifth, children dance round bonfires

Opposite: The Sovereign reveals to her parliamentarians and the nation the plans of her Government as she opens the parliamentary year.

Bonfire Night at Lewes, Sussex is a special occasion and harks back to the reign of Mary Tudor when seventeen Protestants were martyred. Today the memory of those intolerant times is an excuse for a huge bonfire and fireworks display which thousands of people attend.

singing, 'Remember, remember the fifth of November, with Gunpowder, treason and plot'.

The Gunpowder Plot evolved out of the antagonism that existed between Parliament and King James I of England (and VI of Scotland) who had succeeded Elizabeth as Sovereign. At that time, Parliament was trying to establish the new Church of England. In its efforts to bring about religious stability after the Dissolution, Parliament set about expelling Puritans, on the one hand, and fining Catholics who refused to accept the new Church, on the other. It was one of the latter, Robert Catesby, who gathered together a group of Catholics and planned the blowing-up of Parliament – but it was Guy (or Guido) Fawkes, a soldier of fortune, who was caught lighting the fuse. Fawkes, having been caught red-handed, was tortured and hanged as was the custom of the times, and his name has been immortalized by the practice of keeping up the remembrance of the Gunpowder Plot.

Today, the Fifth of November (also known as Bonfire Night) is an excuse for a country-wide burst of incendiary activity. Weeks before, in gardens and in the open spaces of towns and villages, huge piles of wood, old furniture, cardboard boxes, garden cuttings – in fact, anything remotely flammable – start to appear. Meanwhile, shops stock up on boxes of rockets, Roman candles, Vesuvian volcanoes, space missiles, Catherine wheels and other imaginative fireworks. Children make 'Guys' out of old clothes stuffed with newspapers, usually topped with a horrible mask, ready for burning on Bonfire Night. On the fifth, crowds gather round the bonfire, the 'Guy' is burnt, fireworks fill the skies and jacket potatoes are cooked in the bottom of the fires.

In larger cities, or historic places, gigantic Bonfire Night celebrations are put on, with professionals in charge of the spectacular displays which fill

the November night skies. One of these takes place at beautiful Leeds Castle on the edge of the North Downs near Maidstone. Leeds is a privately-owned castle used for conferences and special events, including the Fifth of November. On the night, the fireworks blaze in the sky and are reflected in the broad moat which surrounds the castle – a splendid sight, enhanced by its historic setting.

Spectacular firework displays also take place at Glastonbury, a West Country town to the south-west of the Mendip Hills, in Somerset. Glastonbury is near the celebrated cathedral town of Wells, which also celebrates Bonfire Night, though without the festival procession of its neighbour.

Glastonbury has a magnificent but ruined Abbey. King Arthur and Queen Guinevere are supposedly buried in the Abbey grounds. Overlooking the town is a conical hill, Glastonbury Tor, which legend says was a favourite place of Arthur. Also in Glastonbury is the famous Glastonbury Thorn, which grew from the staff carried by Joseph of Arimathea who, it is said, brought to Glastonbury the chalice used at the Last Supper. The thorn now grows in the grounds of the ruined Abbey and is renowned for its unusual habit of blooming at Christmas time.

The Glastonbury Guy Fawkes Festival is unusually large for a town of its size, and comprises a procession of some 80 decorated floats. The Festival springs from an ancient custom of carrying lighted tar barrels down the steep High Street and the setting alight of tarred rags tied to the railing at the bottom. In 1920 this traditional ritual was expanded by a group of Glastonbury people from Chilkwell Street. At first, the Festival simply consisted of a procession of costumed children, followed by the lighting of a bonfire, but this soon developed into a procession of floats accompanied by bands.

London's Alexandra Palace opened in 1878 and was at one time the headquarters of the B.B.C. It was used for exhibitions until destroyed by fire in 1980 and is now being rebuilt. However, this huge Guy Fawkes Night firework display is still an annual event.

215

Above: Somerset has many fine carnivals and this one at Bridgwater is among the most ambitious with huge illuminated floats and bands.

Below: According to legend, Joseph of Arimathea planted the twig which grew into this thorn tree at Glastonbury's fine ruined abbey.

Today the Festival is a colourful event which attracts some 75,000 people each year, including visitors from overseas. The floats, which represent various themes – King Arthur and His Knights, Space Travel, the Monks of Glastonbury, etc. – are changed from year to year. The procession is illuminated by over 4000 light bulbs, spreading their light over the crowds that line the route to the bonfire, where everyone dances and sings to the accompaniment of the town band. Naturally, on the night of the Festival, the restaurants and pubs of Glastonbury are filled with people out to enjoy themselves. Funds raised on this unusual evening, planned and executed by the people of Glastonbury, are donated to charity.

Among the great pageants of autumn, one of the most popular is the Lord Mayor's Show, a festival for the city of business, commerce and money markets which the Lord Mayor represents.

The position of Lord Mayor of London was created in the 13th century by the much maligned King John. Unlike his hero brother, Richard the Lion Heart, a famous Crusader who spent much of the country's revenues on his military adventures, John was an ambitious and efficient administrator. He concentrated on improvements in civil administration, the law and the exchequer and, as a result, had a good relationship with the businessmen and lawyers of the country, most of whom were found in London. On becoming King after Richard's death, John rewarded his City friends by granting them the right to set up a commune with their own Mayor at its head – a right confirmed by the Magna Carta. Thus the City of London, which preserves its independence to this day, was created. One of the conditions of the charter, however, was that each Mayor of the City, on election, should journey to Westminster to acknowledge his loyalty to the monarch. It is this journey which is re-enacted today when the Lord

Mayor sets off from the Mansion House. Nowadays, the journey stops at the Law Courts, just outside the City Limits, where the Mayor is sworn in by the Lord Chief Justice and the Judges of the Queen's Bench Division, instead of going on to Westminster.

The Lord Mayor's Show is one of the most colourful and picturesque celebrations of the year. It is also one of the best supported; every important City business makes sure that it has a decorated float. Over 130 different groups of marchers and decorated cars move through the City on show day. There are floats entered by all kinds of organizations, including banks, building societies, insurance companies, the Livery Companies (representing the original guilds of different trades), important entertainment organizations etc. In addition, there are groups from the armed services and numerous military, marine and other bands are spaced out along the procession to keep the colour and entertainment going throughout is length. Towards the end of the procession appears the Lord Mayor's coach. This splendid golden affair was built in the 18th century and has painted panels by the Italian painter Cipriani. It is a veritable Cinderella coach suitable for Dick Whittington, who, according to legend, was Lord Mayor of London no less than three times, thanks to the rat-catching ability of his cat!

The great procession starts off from the Guildhall (which dates from the 15th century, when it was the Hall of the Corporation of the City of London) and proceeds down London Wall along the lines of the old Roman Wall to Wood Street. It then turns down Gresham Street, named after the financial adviser to Elizabeth I, towards Bank, the square around which are ranged the Bank of England, the Greek temple-style Royal Exchange and the Corinthian-porticoed Mansion House, residence of the Lord Mayor. From here the procession moves up Poultry, once a market

Everyone connected with London participates in the Lord Mayor's Show including units of the army of today and yesteryear. Here are some of the soldiers of Cromwellian times.

for fowls, and Cheapside, where the great tower of Bow Church stands. At St. Paul's Cathedral the Lord Mayor descends from his coach to receive a blessing from the Dean of Wren's finest Renaissance masterpiece, and to hear an anthem sung by the choir. From the Cathedral there is a slow descent down Ludgate Hill to Ludgate Circus, under which runs the channelled course of the River Fleet. The procession then climbs Fleet Street, with St. Brides, another beautiful Wren church, on the left and the offices of famous newspapers on each side. On the left, at the top of Fleet Street, is Prince Henry's Room, all that remains of a Tudor building from before the Fire of London, and opposite is St. Dunstan's Church, with an effigy of Queen Elizabeth I made during her lifetime. Ahead loom the gothic walls and pinnacles of the Law Courts.

The Lord Mayor enters the Law Courts at about midday and promises, before the Lord Chief Justice, the Master of the Rolls and other dignitaries, to perform his duties as Lord Mayor.

The return journey to Guildhall begins after a short break, with the procession now taking a route along the River Thames – past the ships *Chrysanthemum*, *President* and *Wellington* moored along the Victoria Embankment and stopping at the riverside of the Inner and Middle Temples to greet old soldiers and members of the Royal Navy Reserve who offer the new Lord Mayor a tot of rum before he returns to the City.

The evening of the Lord Mayor's Show concludes with a splendid banquet in the Mansion House and, for the public, a spectacular firework display from a barge moored in the Thames which lights up London's riverside in an unforgettable show of blazing colour.

Autumn's most solemn occasion is Remembrance Day. There is little colourful pageantry during this ceremony, which remembers the $2\frac{1}{2}$ million dead of two World Wars, but it is a moving occasion and one

Opposite top: The gold Lord Mayor's carriage gives a fairy-tale touch to the show that evokes the legendary times of Dick Whittington and his cat.

Opposite bottom: Mounted hussars ride proudly ahead of the Lord Mayor cheered by vast crowds of British and overseas visitors who habitually line the procession route.

Below: The Lord Mayor's show ends fittingly with a dazzling firework display on the Thames with floodlit St. Paul's Cathedral providing a memorable background.

which is an essential element of the British year. Formerly called Armistice Day and celebrated on the day the First World War ended, 11 November, Remembrance Sunday has now taken on a wider significance as a ceremonial of remembrance for all who died in both World Wars, as well as other conflicts: a time for meditation on the failure of human beings to live in peace and harmony.

The Cenotaph, a plain stone monolith in the centre of Whitehall designed by Sir Edwin Lutyens, is the focal point of the ceremony. Around it stand detachments of the armed forces: the Royal Navy, the Royal Marines, the Army, the Royal Air Force, the Territorial and Army Volunteer Reserves, and the Royal Auxiliary Air Force. Also present are detachments of civilian men and women who have served either in the two World Wars or other theatres of conflict. Massed bands provide sombre accompaniment throughout the ceremony – except for the moment of remembrance itself, when silence reigns.

The moment for reflection occurs at exactly 11.00 a.m., after the arrival of the royal party from Buckingham Palace. As the Queen and her group take their places before the Cenotaph, Big Ben solemnly strikes the hour and one single gun shot is heard from the Horse Guards Parade. Two minutes silence ensues, broken only by the restless movement of a horse or the fluttering of pigeons.

To a large proportion of the population, the conflicts of the two World Wars are merely history – something that happened before they were born. But few who witness that motionless moment of silence and the laying of the wreaths at the Cenotaph can fail to be moved by the occasion. An occasion which transcends national boundaries in an expression of grief for the millions of men, women and children who died in the conflicts.

The pageantry of autumn is also represented by an air show which is

Opposite: A sober moment in the busy turmoil of London's year is experienced on Remembrance Day in November when homage is paid to the victims of war.

Below: The Queen lays her wreath at the Cenotaph, a simple stone monument in Whitehall, on Remembrance Day.

held in England and France on alternate years. When it is Britain's turn it is held at Farnborough. The Farnborough Show has a distinctive character, evident at first glance as one looks down from the slopes which provide good viewing of the airfield. From here the Farnborough Show looks like a medieval tournament, a kind of Field of the Cloth of Gold, for the stands are not concrete buildings, but marquees and tents gaily decked in flags and pennants, in striking contrast to the modern aircraft which are parked about the field.

Farnborough is primarily a trade show where all the latest developments in aerospace are shown off to customers who will spend some £800 million at the exhibition. Accordingly, the first few days are devoted to business, but the show is then opened to the public, who arrive in vast numbers, often in family groups led by fathers and sons whose enthusiasm for the most up-to-date aircraft and equipment provides the motivation for the visit.

In the morning the displays are crowded with visitors examining the products on show. A major attraction is the open static display of aircraft, including combat aircraft, the chunky looking Harriers with their powerful jets, the sleek Tornados and Jaguars. Then there are helicopters, observation aircraft, air freighters and passenger aircraft in dazzling variety. Many of these are not only visible from the outside, but can be entered and examined from the interior.

Five covered halls provide accommodation for display stands where all the components of the show aircraft can be examined in detail. Here there are powerful jet and turbo-prop engines, hydraulic braking systems, electronic navigation systems, satellites, missiles and every other imaginable innovation in aerospace. In addition to the static displays there are also air-borne exhibitions, with special demonstrations by the Red Devils and fly-pasts by such celebrities of the world of flight as Spitfire and Concorde.

Pageantry is not too far-fetched an expression for the Farnborough Air Show, for it has all the colour, excitement and historical background of a pageant. Indeed, the first shows at Hendon were actually described as pageants. At these shows, which took place in the 1930s, only a few aircraft were displayed and the trade part of the show was something of an afterthought. Farnborough was first used in 1948 and has continued to develop and extend its range as the years have gone by, so that today it accommodates some 800 companies and over 350,000 visitors at every show and provides a festival atmosphere that is hard to beat.

THE END OF AUTUMN

Autumn is a two-stage season, beginning in the wake of summer, when it seems that the leaves will linger on the trees and the chrysanthemums and Michaelmas daisies will continue to bloom for ever. In a few weeks, however, the winds and rain arrive to loosen the last golden leaves and flood the riverside fields. The first frost turns the last green plants brown and causes much early morning activity as commuters scrape at the frosted windscreens of their cars. In the country the trees are seen in a new stark beauty, their branch and twig structures making a delicate tracery against the wind-blown skies. In the cities, the buildings and traffic form a kind of *son et lumière* show of flashing signs and weaving car lights, with silhouettes of people hurrying from work or pausing before bright shop windows.

In autumn the great indoor spectacles begin, and among the first of these is the Horse of the Year Show at Wembley. One of the most popular equestrian events of the year, it is not only a test of horsemanship and horses, but also an entertainment which appeals even to those who do not see a horse again for the rest of the year.

The first night of the show is a gala night, with the accent on fun rather than serious competition, and the proceeds of this colourful evening are donated to charity. On day two the serious business of the show begins, with an all-day programme taking place in the arena and outside rings. Various heats eliminate all but the horses that will compete in the finals.

The Show's events are many and varied, with competitions for novice and professional jumpers, speed events and the famous puissance competition, when horses have to jump formidable heights to win. There is a competition to find the Police Horse of the Year, demonstrating the discipline and control of horse and rider when faced with such distractions as traffic, football crowds, boisterous revellers and other hazards of a

The triple jump at the Horse of the Year Show is one of the tests of horse and rider at this popular equestrian event at Wembley.

Children's Pony Clubs prepare all during the summer for their big moment at the Horse of the Year Show.

mounted policeman's life. The Personalities Parade is a popular item, in which the famous horses and riders of the year can be seen. There are also scurry driving contests, riding club quadrilles and the children's events in which Pony Clubs from all over Britain compete.

The show ends on a high note, with a final night where horses and riders representing every kind of equestrian activity in the country appear; a stirring occasion, it is made the more so by the presence of the trumpeters of the Household Cavalry, military bands and many of the leading personalities of the horse world.

Another show that makes its appearance on the threshold of winter is the Royal Smithfield Show. Here, the farming skills of Britain, which have continued to develop scientifically, but have perhaps been pushed backstage by the razzle-dazzle of industrial enterprise, are displayed. The show has its roots in the 12th century, when a cattle market first operated

at West Smithfield in the City of London, but nowadays is held at Earls' Court Exhibition Centre.

In medieval times Smithfield was the place where farmers drove their cattle for sale to the London markets and it was also the site of a notorious rough-and-tumble fair. Scurvy knaves preyed on the crowds that came to buy or to watch the strolling shows. People also came to Smithfield to watch the executions that took place there. The Scottish leader William Wallace and the rebellious Wat Tyler, as well as many innocent victims of religious persecution, met their end at Smithfield, watched by ghoulish crowds. Smithfield still retains much of its medieval interest and continues its daily life as a cattle market. Facing it is St. Bartholomew's Hospital, founded by a courtier of Henry I who also founded the Church of St. Bartholomew the Great, across the square, the finest and second oldest medieval church in London.

The modern Royal Smithfield Show is a vast trading fair where livestock are bought and sold and modern farm machinery is demonstrated. It is also an opportunity that few Londoners miss to learn something about the mechanics of modern farming. Town-dwellers can see the best prize specimens of cattle, sheep and pigs and learn much about the quality of the cuts that are on sale at butcher's shops. At Smithfield, the reality of the raising of livestock and its ultimate fate is not disguised, and many of the prize specimens are seen both alive and on the hook – a transformation that may upset the squeamish and confirm vegetarians in their principles.

Whatever one's feelings, there is no doubt that the Royal Smithfield Show is a spectacular event, and if it brings home the realities of life and death it could be said to be appropriate for this time of the year. Nature appears to die as winter approaches and human optimism and *joie de vivre* needs the festival of Christmas to keep it buoyed up.

Judging cattle at the impressive Royal Smithfield Show in London, a showcase for livestock and farm machinery.

227

A Winter of Delights

A hundred years ago the onset of winter brought everyday life almost to a standstill or, at best, reduced activity to a snail's pace. This was especially true in the countryside, where there was neither electricity to provide instant domestic light, nor good roads to make access to nearby towns and cities easy. Even in the towns, electricity was still a novelty, motor cars still experimental and the telephone line from London to Paris had only just been laid. London was lit by gaslight then and few ventured out into the dark streets, often totally enveloped in murky fogs, unless they had their own carriage or could afford to hire a hansom cab. There was, of course, a winter season for those who belonged to high society; there were balls in the splendid mansions of Belgravia and hunting

The Christmas tree presented by Norway to Britain every year in memory of wartime comradeship stands proudly in Trafalgar Square.

on the estates of the landed gentry. If the weather became insupportable, there was always the French Riviera, where all the best people gathered to await the spring. But for ordinary folk, winter was a time for drawing the curtains and huddling round the fire.

Even during the first quarter of the 20th century, winter was a period of withdrawal for all except those who lived in the big cities who could venture out occasionally to the theatre, a restaurant, or to those new places of popular entertainment – the cinema and the palais de dance.

Since the Second World War all that has changed. Today, Britain cheers up winter with national and international shows, sporting events ranging from ice skating to snooker championships and a vast variety of other entertainments, from discos to dog shows.

The centre of 'show business Britain' is London, where winter activities begin with the preparations for the celebration of Christmas even before the ashes of Bonfire Night have gone cold.

THE CHRISTMAS CELEBRATIONS

Once upon a time, the winter solstice was a time for meditation on the year gone by and of hope for the year to come. The sun, giver of life, was at its

'The Gold Diggers', one of the spectacular scenes from the ice show extravaganza 'Holiday on Ice' held at London's Wembley Arena.

lowest ebb and ancient people, lacking the scientific knowledge we have today, feared that its power to spread life over the earth might never return. Midwinter was thus a season of death, but also a season of hope – a concept later embodied in the Christian faith. By the 19th century, the religious side of Christmas was paramount in people's minds at the time of the winter solstice – although the celebration of Christmas still included some of the pagan symbolism and ritual of the pre-Christian era. The Christmas tree, representing the spirit of nature, became the centre of every home, and the yule log burnt in most grates to honour the ancient gods who ordered the movements of the sun. The mistletoe was hung up, though the discreet kisses it invited were a far cry from its Druid ancestry, when it was considered a sacred plant with miraculous healing powers and a symbol of fertility.

In this century the Christian significance of the winter solstice has been overlaid with that of the Roman Saturnalia, a period of unbridled enjoyment, which even the slaves were allowed to share. Christmas today is a strange and rich mixture of spiritual contemplation and a natural desire for enjoyment and self-indulgence. So on the one hand, there are large congregations at church services, charitable donations increase and quarrels are ended. On the other, there is Christmas shopping, theatrical entertainments, packed restaurants and much eating, drinking and making merry.

The centre of all this activity, which begins in November and carries on until January, is London – though the show is echoed in every town and village throughout Britain. London is the hub of celebrations which attract not only people from all over Britain, but from Europe and beyond.

London's Christmas starts with the appearance of exceptionally well-designed store windows, often a show in themselves, with tableaux representing popular Christmas themes, children's stories or wintry scenes with falling snow, reindeers and robins. The signal for the Christmas shopping spree to begin is given when the illuminations are turned on in Oxford Street, Regent Street and Bond Street: Angels fly through the air,

Above: London's stores add to the Christmas atmosphere with appropriate window displays. This one at Selfridges depicts a scene from Kenneth Grahame's classic children's book The Wind in the Willows.

Opposite: Christmas lights illuminate the shopping streets of London every December and attract shoppers from all over the country to London's West End.

Father Christmases dance above the December traffic and lights wink and sparkle on the bare boughs of the pavement trees. Street hawkers offer merchandise at unheard-of bargain prices or sell Christmas fruit imported from faraway places.

Among these commercial trappings, much of the old spirit of Christmas survives. For example, there are the pantomimes, carrying on the traditions of medieval mummers' plays. The Christmas crib makes its appearance in most churches and many homes. Carol services form the basis of many beautiful musical celebrations at Christmas time. Also, and perhaps surprisingly in this age of disbelief, the Father Christmas legend still survives in family homes and in many department stores.

Among the carol services, one of the most moving is performed in King's College Chapel, Cambridge where, on Christmas Eve, the Festival of Nine Lessons and Carols is held. The beautiful and simple interior of this lovely chapel is crowded on this great occasion. As the choristers arrive in their bright red cassocks and white surplices, there is a tense air of expectation which lasts until a chosen chorister breaks into 'Once in Royal David's City' – his clear treble voice floating above the candle-lit congregation and rising to the fan vaulting above the choir stalls.

Another great Christmas experience is provided at Norwich Cathedral, an impressive Norman building whose spire soars 40 m (135 ft) over the flat Norfolk farmlands. Here the carol service includes a touching ritual, the Christingle, in which candles inserted into oranges are gradually lit until the whole cathedral is bright with flickering light.

A different kind of carol service, with more recent connections, is the one conducted in London at Trafalgar Square, where a tall Christmas tree, presented by Norway to commemorate wartime comradeship and sacrifice of the Norwegian and British peoples, is erected every year. Here,

The ritual of Christingle, a favourite Christmas service with children, is carried out at many of Britain's cathedrals and churches. The candles are lit from one single flame and distributed through the congregation as a symbolic gesture of brotherhood.

at the northern side of the square, in front of the National Gallery and near the Church of St. Martin in-the-Fields, the crowds gather to visit the Christmas crib and watch the lights on the tree being switched on. Trafalgar Square, built at the suggestion of the great Regency architect Nash, is also the scene of festive gatherings on New Year's Eve, when its Lutyens fountains were once the scene of damp revels, but are now fitted with wooden covers.

SHOW TIME

December is a popular month for the opera and ballet, with special shows at Christmas. The Royal Opera House, Covent Garden, is filled with families who come to see such enduring ballet classics as the *Nutcracker* and *Swan Lake*. Though difficult to book, for Covent Garden seats only some 2000 people, there is no better place to see the ballet than in E. M. Barry's rococo Victorian masterpiece, with its ornate plaster work and red plush atmosphere. After the performance visitors can enjoy another show – that of the converted Covent Garden Market, a marvellous enclave of restaurants, wine bars, shops, stalls and itinerant entertainers.

Nearby, in St. Martin's Lane, is the popular Coliseum. The theatre was built in 1904 as a music hall by Sir Oswald Stoll, whose architect erected the glass globe which gives the building its idiosyncratic appearance. During its Edwardian period the Coliseum featured such famous or notorious stars of the stage as Ellen Terry, Sarah Bernhardt and Lily Langtry. Later, when music hall lost its appeal, the theatre became a cinema and had a chequered career until 1968, when it became the home of the Sadler's Wells Opera Company, later to become the English National Opera, whose repertoire, sung in English, is more varied and less traditional in approach than the Royal Opera.

The spirit of Christmas is celebrated in London's Trafalgar Square with carol singing by the illuminated Christmas tree.

A Christmas show which has become established as a part of the Christmas tradition is the ever-popular Nutcracker *ballet with music by Tchaikovsky.*

Another famous theatre which has a popular Christmas season is Sadler's Wells at the Angel, Islington – once a spa where Londoners took the waters during the 18th century. Visitors to the original theatre were entertained by the famous Grimaldi clowns and, in the 19th century, Samuel Phelps produced some 34 of Shakespeare's plays there. The popularity of Islington declined towards the end of the century and the spa and theatre suffered an eclipse. The elegant 18th-century houses fell into decay but, in recent years, new life has been breathed into Islington and many of its squares are much sought-after residential areas. The theatre was completely rebuilt and reopened in 1931. The outstanding success of the ballet company under Ninette de Valois and the opera company under Lilian Baylis led to their being acknowledged as unofficial 'national' companies; the ballet moved to the Royal Opera House where it was given a Royal Charter in 1956, and the opera moved to the Coliseum. Today, Sadler's Wells continues to receive plenty of support from lovers of the opera and dance who go to seasons presented regularly there by top British and international companies.

The most traditional of all Christmas shows is the pantomime, a uniquely English form of theatrical entertainment which was invented in the 19th century by John Rich. There had been theatrical entertainments at Christmas since medieval times, however, originating from the mummers' plays which were displays of dancing and singing by masked performers. The players travelled from house to house, collecting alms, entertaining and being entertained by the householders. The central theme of the mumming play is the triumph of Good, personified by St. George, over Evil in the shape of a dragon. The performances were quite spontaneous and there was no written script, the words and music being passed on by word of mouth from one generation to another. In the 15th century, the mummers' performance became more formalized, with a proper plot and written dialogue in rhyming couplets. Other characters were introduced and often, instead of St. George, there would be Robin Hood or some other popular hero; Evil was the devil himself, Beelzebub, who was often made into a figure of fun, arousing both hisses and laughter from the audience.

Alongside the mummers' plays there were Nativity plays or miracle plays, telling the story of Christmas in a simple way to country folk. These were often sponsored by the monastic orders and parish churches. Sometimes the plays, acted on farm wagons in market squares, would last all day and cover not only the Nativity, but scenes from many other books in the Bible.

In the early days, traditional Christmas theatre was performed on two levels – one for the Court and the high born and the other for the common people. During Tudor times, the play acting at Court came to be called the masque – a sophisticated entertainment often written by leading playwrights such as Ben Jonson – but the mummers' plays or miracle plays continued, being renamed morality plays after the Reformation.

When John Rich arrived on the scene there had been a considerable change in the social structure in England. The merchant class had long since grown into what was later to be known as the middle class, and England was becoming a rich nation able to support a permanent theatrical establishment. John Rich chose the Lincoln's Inn Theatre for his first work, combining some of the characteristics of a mummers' play with those of a masque, including elements of the Italian *Commedia del Arte*. The play was called *Harlequin Executed* and told a story of a fairy queen who turned the characters of a harlequinade into real people, and of the love of Harlequin for Columbine. Rich introduced both dramatic and

The pantomime is a traditional British entertainment at Christmas time. A favourite is Jack and the Beanstalk, *which includes the comic pantomime cow, here staged at the Richmond Theatre in Surrey.*

Above: Schools and church groups often include a Nativity play in their Christmas celebrations. This one was performed by the Rosary School of Hampstead, North London.

Right: The Marshfield Mummers perform at the small village of Marshfield in the western Cotswolds on Boxing Day and wear costumes made of daily newspapers.

comic characters into his play, the latter being played by the famous family of clowns, the Grimaldis.

Since then, many pantomimes have come into being, all based on simple fairy stories such as 'Babes in the Wood', 'Cinderella', 'Puss in Boots', etc. All the pantomimes embody the idea of life as a conflict between Good, personified by the hero and the Good Fairy, and Evil, in the shape of wicked barons, robbers, ugly sisters, giants and so on.

Despite its ancient form and simple concept the pantomime is still immensely popular throughout Britain and the cheers of the audience for protagonists of Good and boos for the forces of Evil ring out from theatres all over the country.

Once the Christmas celebrations are over, it is time to welcome the New Year. Throughout Britain, parties take place in private and public places; in Scotland Hogmanay is a national celebration during which much whisky is consumed and there is dancing and carousing into the 'wee hours'. At midnight, people link hands to sing 'Auld Lang Syne' and exchange kisses to welcome the New Year, and the tradition of first-footing is celebrated – the first dark-haired person who crosses the threshold at midnight brings good luck.

Another celebration near to New Year commemorates Robert Burns' birthday. The 25th of January, Burns Night, is celebrated all over Scotland and wherever Scots are gathered world-wide. It consists of a ritual dinner eaten in the poet's honour with drams of whisky to help it down.

The ritual is a picturesque and colourful occasion as it provides an opportunity to wear the tartan and to celebrate in true Scottish fashion. The main event of the evening is the breathtaking moment when the haggis is piped into the hall. The haggis, a sheep's stomach stuffed with spiced meats and regarded by most Scots as a great national delicacy, arrives on a

Robbie Burns is one of the best loved poets and his warm human spirit is appropriately celebrated at Burns Night parties that commemmorate his birth.

The World Travel Market at London's Olympia held to promote tourism, brings together countries from all over the world, and many of them present colourful shows of their national songs and dances.

Pedigree Long-haired, Short-haired, Foreign and Oriental cats all mingle at the annual National Cat Club Show at Olympia.

silver platter born aloft by haggis bearers while a piper plays, the music having a strange heart-stirring effect on the diners. The haggis is taken to the guest of honour who then stabs it while reciting Burns' famous 'Address to the Haggis', which begins:

Fair fa' your honest sonsie face,
Great Chieftain o' the Puddin'-race . . .

The wounded haggis is then sprinkled with soothing drops of malt whisky and, accompanied by bashed neeps, it is eaten with gusto by the assembled company. The evening ends with speeches in honour of the poet and with Scottish reels which go on far into the night.

THE BIG EXHIBITIONS

The last months of the old year and the first months of the new one are busy times and the streets of the big cities and towns of Britain are crowded with shoppers seeking bargains in the January sales. Many of the visitors who come for the shopping also stay for the big exhibitions that take place in London's great exhibition centres of Earl's Court and Olympia.

The International World Travel Market is held at Olympia and is a vast

showcase for the ever-expanding holiday business. The market, which began a few years ago as a trade fair for companies and countries involved in the travel business, has become a popular public show. Holiday companies vie with each other for custom, providing entertainment and giving away colourful brochures to attract the 20 million Britons who travel abroad each year. The vast central hall of Olympia and its upper level gallery are turned into a colourful fairground with non-stop entertainment; there are Caribbean steel bands, Austrian folk dancers, Mexican mariachi bands, Swiss yodellers, German 'oompah' bands, Spanish flamenco groups and a host of other displays. The stands vary from year to year. You might see a replica of the famous Treetops Hotel in Kenya, facsimiles of Indian temples, a model of the Eiffel Tower or other famous tourist landmarks. Throughout the show, competitions are held for holiday prizes and teams of representatives of countries from all parts of the world give out advice and information from their stands.

In December, Olympia is the home of the world's largest cat show, organized by the National Cat Club which was formed in 1887. Some 2000 cats are entered in the show, accompanied by the owners who present a varied and interesting cross-section of the world of cat lovers. Retired generals and their wives, Greenham Common ladies, actresses and policemen are all brought together by their common attachment to cats.

The great hall at Olympia presents a remarkable spectacle while the show is in progress. Thousands of wire cages contain every imaginable kind of cat: long-haired and short-haired cats, single-coloured and multi-coloured ones, smooth-haired varieties and curly-haired ones, round 'cobby' shaped cats and those that are long and lean in appearance. Then there are different races of cats: Abyssinian, Balinese, Burmese, Korat, Siamese and Turkish, including the fluffy Angoras. During the show there are 26 veterinary surgeons in attendance, and 20 judges who decide on the Grand Champion of the show as well as the winners in each of the many categories.

Alongside the rows of cages the owners can be seen trying to cheer up the bored cats which would much rather be at home in front of the fire or watching the world pass by from a window seat. Nearby are stalls selling every kind of cat food and accessory, including diamanté studded combs and collars, smart tartan winter coats and fur bootees.

The Crufts Dog Show takes place at Earl's Court in February and is a

Champion dogs impress by their intelligence as much as by their looks at the Crufts Dog Show launched by Charles Crufts in 1891 and held each year in London.

In the midst of winter there comes a vision of summer at the artificial harbour at the London International Boat Show.

very different kind of event. Unlike cats, dogs are eager to please and enjoy showing off their talents.

The Crufts Dog Show was launched by Charles Cruft in 1891 after a visit to Paris, where he organized a dog show for French dog breeders as part of the Paris Exhibition. Fired by the idea of holding such an event in England, Cruft hired the Royal Agricultural Hall in Islington and organized a show which continued annually until his death in 1938. The show was then taken over by the Kennel Club, which was founded in 1873. The Kennel Club keeps a helpful eye on the 4000 dog shows held in Britain every year and has among its aims the promotion of improvement in conditions at dog shows, trials, obedience tests, etc. It also classifies breeds, registers pedigrees and generally interests itself in the efficient regulating of everything to do with dogs.

The popular standing of the Crufts Show is evident from the large entry. There are representatives from every conceivable breed of dog, classed in six basic groups: terrier, working dogs, utility dogs, hounds, toy dogs and gun dogs. Throughout the day the dogs sit and lie in their appointed stalls – some sleepy, some restlessly active, many of them giving voice to their boredom – awaiting the call to the judging rings. They will be looked over by judges who are specialists in their category and will be checked for the points and tested for their obedience. Having proved best in its class, the winning dog then competes in the final competition against the best dogs in every other group, with a chance of earning the title of best in the show.

For its visitors the Crufts Dog show presents a scene of constant activity. The dogs move about in their own pens and stalls while a non-stop show takes place in the rings, where police dogs show their intelligence and courage, guide dogs demonstrate their infinite patience and good sense, gun dogs their persistence and gentleness and puppies have their own competition, showing off their irresistible charms.

Another show that everyone always enjoys is the London International Boat Show at Olympia, a colourful occasion which takes place at a time when the weather outside is at its most cheerless. One of the delights of this annual show, which has been going for 33 years at the time of writing, is the little harbour which is created in the centre of the hall. Filled with craft, it gives the impression of one of those tiny West Country villages which are crowded with people who mess about in boats in the summer. Here at the Boat Show you can see every kind of boat from giant cruiser to tiny dinghy; and there is something for everyone, from the amateur sailor who rarely ventures more than a quarter of a mile off shore to the yachtsmen who take part in the Fastnet Race.

Most years the Boat Show has a theme; in 1987 it was the project known as Chelsea Harbour, a yachting marina that will be built in London itself at Chelsea Reach and will have some of the most expensive and desirable accommodation in the City of Westminster around it. Most years, too, there are a series of entertainments planned beside the yachting pool. There are fashion shows, acrobatic and other displays, and in other parts of the show there are exhibitions of marine paintings, of models of ships of the Royal Navy and demonstrations of sub-aqua diving. There is often a

The attractive North Entrance of St. James's Palace, a picturesque brick building which encloses several courtyards, open to the public.

famous boat on display such as, in 1987, the *African Queen*, the star of the film, which was built in England in 1912.

ANCIENT TRADITIONS OF WINTER

A charming and little known ceremony of winter time is the Epiphany Service held at St. James's Chapel in the palace built by Henry VIII by St. James's Park. The Epiphany Service originated in the 16th century, when St. James's was the main royal palace, and takes place on the anniversary of the three Kings' arrival at Bethlehem, carrying gold, myrrh and frankincense to offer to the baby Jesus. Up until the time of the Hanoverian kings the monarch was always present at the Epiphany service. The service is now conducted by the Bishop of London on behalf of the Queen. As a reminder of the times when there was a royal presence at the ceremony, the service is attended by the Yeomen of the Guard who once came to protect the monarch, dressed in their splendid Tudor uniforms. To complement the Yeomen, the boy choristers, descendants of the choirs that sang for Henry V at Agincourt and accompanied Henry VIII to meet the French King, Francis I, at the Field of the Cloth of Gold, wear Tudor tunics in scarlet and gold. The men of the choir wear red cassocks and white surplices.

It is an intimate ceremony, to which only a few members of the public are admitted due to the limited seating in the chapel. The service, like Maundy Thursday, is an occasion on which an offering of gold, frankincense and myrrh is made on behalf of the monarch. The gold is in the form of 25 sovereigns. The gifts are handed by the Gentlemen Ushers to the Dean of the Chapels Royal who accepts and blesses the gifts. The gold will be changed into modern currency and distributed among charities supported by St. James's Chapel. The frankincense and myrrh will be used to make incense for High Anglican churches.

The Tower of London, whose White Tower was built for William the Conqueror, preserves such ancient traditions as the Ceremony of the Keys, carried out every evening by the Warders.

The chapel, which has been the scene of many royal weddings including those of William and Mary, Queen Anne, George IV, Queen Victoria and George V, is one of the few remaining parts of the building erected by Henry VIII. The Chapel was built in 1531 and it was in the 16th century that the monarchy decided to create a permanent royal residence with a more pleasant atmosphere than the Tower of London, the previous royal home. Perhaps this is not surprising, for the medieval history of the Tower, first built by William the Conqueror, is a grim tale. The Tower, surrounded by defensive walls and towers during the reigns of Richard I and Henry III, was a royal fortress where the court lived as well as a prison and place of torture and execution. William Wallace was imprisoned there, and the Duke of Clarence was murdered, according to legend, by being drowned in a butt of Malmsey wine. One of the worst crimes to take place in the fortress was the murder of the Princes in the Tower, which was attributed to Richard III. Among other executions carried out in the gloomy fortress over the centuries were those of Anne Boleyn and Katherine Howard, both wives of Henry VIII, Lady Jane Grey and her husband, Lord Dudley, Sir Thomas More, Bishop Fisher, the Earl of Essex, Sir Walter Raleigh, and many other less notable individuals who were imprisoned and tortured in the dark dungeons.

Despite, or perhaps because of, its murky history, the Tower is a popular place with visitors to London. The entrance is over a drawbridge, passing through the Middle Tower and over the moat, past the Bell Tower and the Bloody Tower. Below the Bloody Tower, down by the River Thames, is Traitor's Gate, through which prisoners arriving by boat entered the Tower. The central court contains the White Tower. It is surrounded by lawns on which the ravens strut, passing the site of the scaffold where so many met their deaths. To the north of the White Tower are the Waterloo Barracks, built by the Duke of Wellington, where the closely-guarded Crown Jewels are kept.

The Tower is open all year round and its ceremonies are carried out every day. In summer it is very crowded, so there is a good deal to be said for making a winter visit, when even the weather seems to add to the atmosphere of grimness and doom that hangs over much of the building.

One of the most evocative ceremonies concerns the keys used to lock the Tower gates at night. This takes place at ten minutes to ten every evening and it has continued in the same format for over 700 years. Tickets for this ceremony can be obtained by applying to the Governor of the Tower of London.

The ritual begins when the Chief Yeoman, dressed in his Tudor uniform of scarlet coat and black hat, emerges from the Byward Tower to join an escort of guards. The group, led by one of the guards holding a lantern, carries out a tour of inspection, strolling slowly between the dark walls, past the towers that loom up in the darkness silhouetted against the glow of the city. At the Bloody Tower, haunted, it is said, by the ghost of Anne Boleyn, a sentry calls out the same challenge that was made in Tudor times:

'Halt! Who goes there?'

'The keys', answers the Chief Yeoman.

'Whose keys?'

'Queen Elizabeth's keys.'

'Pass Queen Elizabeth's keys, all's well.'

The group then marches up the Broad Walk where the guards present arms and the Chief Warder cries out, 'God preserve Queen Elizabeth', just as he did when the first Elizabeth was on the throne. Finally, the last post is sounded and the guard dismissed.

A ceremony such as this, repeated nightly for over 700 years – through

times of peace and war – is a valuable reminder of the continuity essential to the evolution of a national culture, linking the England of the Tudors with that of the present day.

Another ancient festival which, like the Epiphany Service, takes place around Twelfth Night is the Whittlesea Straw Bear Festival. The town, now called Whittlesey, lies to the east of the cathedral city of Peterborough. This unusual event, traditionally taking place on the first Monday after Twelfth Night (Plough Monday), has recently been revived and includes many historic aspects of country celebrations. The event is based around the age-old custom of dressing up a ploughman in straw, to represent a living corn dolly. The best straw from the previous harvest was stored away especially for this occasion and from this arose a saying, still in existence, that anything put aside for best 'will do for the bear'.

The Bear Festival consists of a procession around the town, from pub to pub, where the bear and its entourage are met by crowds and entertained by singing and dancing. Among the dance performances that take place during the Straw Bear Festival are sword dances based on the traditions of North Yorkshire, Durham and Northumberland, clog dancing from the north-west of England, Morris dancing from the Leicester region and Cotswold dancing. There is a grand Barn Dance on the Saturday night, preceding the Blessing of the Plough after young farmers have dragged it all round the town on the Sunday.

The Tower Guard or Yeoman Warders, popularly known as Beefeaters, wear historic costume said to date from the time of Henry VII.

Above: The Flamborough Sword Dancers appear on the streets of Flamborough in Humberside around Christmas time. Sword dance rituals are performed in several parts of England but their origin is obscure.

Right: This dangerous-looking torch is a clavie, a Scottish version of a burning tar barrel. At Burghead the embers of the clavie are used for starting up hearth fires for good luck.

The association of harvesting, ploughing and Epiphany suggests that the Straw Bear Festival has roots that go back to the very beginnings of agricultural life in Britain. The origins of many of these ancient ceremonies are now forgotten, but they continue to be acknowledged in rituals only understood, perhaps, in the subconscious areas of the national psyche.

One of these is the mysterious ritual of the Burning of the Clavie. This is observed at Burghead, a small fishing port on the east coast of Scotland, on January 12 – the New Year of the ancient calendar. On the night of the twelfth, the townspeople gather and split a tar barrel into two. Each part is nailed to a pole, filled with firewood and set alight. The flaming clavies are then carried around the town, accompanied by the Clavie King and the townspeople. Stops are made at the houses of town dignitaries, who are given pieces of the flaming clavie for good luck. The firelit procession then moves towards the darkness of a headland outside the village, where the clavie is set on the ground. All manner of combustible materials are piled

onto the clavie, and eventually a great bonfire is blazing on the clifftop, overlooking the sea across which the Norsemen, who may have brought this custom with them, came in their longboats.

In the next stage of the ritual the clavie bonfire is pushed downhill, sparkling and sputtering like a giant fireball, while all the townspeople follow it to gather up burning fragments. These they take home to light fires in their own hearths, to ensure good fortune for the coming year. This superstition suggests that the burning clavie ritual is associated with the ancient fire festivals connected with sun gods, probably the most ancient of pagan religious customs.

At Lerwick, capital of the Shetland Islands, the Up-Helly-A' Vikings – 'Guisers' – celebrate their mid-winter festival with a magnificent torch-bearing procession which culminates in the burning of the Viking galley.

VIKING WINTER

Of all the festivals that take place in the dark months at the beginning of the year, the most spectacular are the Viking festivals held at Lerwick, Shetland, and at the cathedral city of York.

The Vikings arrived in Scotland in about A.D. 700, having made the voyage across the North Sea in their beautiful longships. At first there were few Norse visitors and often the object of their journey was to destroy the pirate lairs hidden along the Scottish coasts. Later, the Norsemen began to settle in the north of Scotland, gradually extending their sway to other areas. Among the earliest of the Norse rulers was Thorfinn the Mighty who, it is thought, may have sided with Macbeth against the Scottish King.

When Viking kings and warriors died their bodies were sent to sea in a fiery boat, from which their spirits would make the journey to Valhalla, the heaven of the warriors. The re-enactment of this ceremony is the high spot of the festivals at both Lerwick and York.

At Lerwick a huge procession of Shetlanders in full costume and carrying flaming torches takes the Viking galley to a large field where they form a circle around it. A bugle call is given, and when the last note has sounded the torches are hurled into the galley.

The Lerwick 'Up Helly A' Vikings' also participate in the festival at York, where they join the Jorvik Vikings in the boat-burning ceremony. However, this is only a part of the York festival, which lasts for over four weeks.

York is a beautiful city which has retained much of the architecture of its ancient past. A stone wall, dating from the reign of Edward III, encircles most of the city. Near the confluence of the rivers Foss and Ouse stands the Clifford Tower on a steep conical mound, all that survives of the old castle. Inside the northern quarter of the walls is the Minster, the largest of English medieval churches and one of the most beautiful, with superb stained glass. To the south of the cathedral is an area of narrow streets and houses with overhanging upper storeys, filled with small shops. Nearby is a busy market in a square also surrounded by ancient houses. Extensive gardens stretch along the north and west walls and there are fine buildings along the river, including the 15th-century Guildhall, which was rebuilt after bomb damage in 1942.

During the Viking festival many of the old parts of the city are used as the settings for different events. A spectacular firework display takes place on the Clifford Tower, where William the Conqueror raised his first wooden bailey. A Viking feast is held at the 14th-century Merchant Adventurers Hall on the River Foss. Viking battles and wrestling take place at the Castle and Viking processions march through various parts of the city. The River Ouse is the scene of a Viking longboat race and is also the venue of the grand finale when the Viking funeral is re-enacted after a torchlight procession through the city by the Jorvik Vikings and the wild, bearded Norsemen who have arrived from Lerwick to contribute to the revelry and drama of this unique festival.

CHINESE NEW YEAR

While Vikings remind the British of the ancient ties that link Scandinavia to Britain, in the south of England a more recent relationship is celebrated.

The Jorvik Viking Festival is a month-long celebration of the ancient festival of Jolablot – *which heralded the coming of the New Year and survival through the bitter winter. Jorvik was the Viking name for York when the city was under Viking rule 1000 years ago.*

In the depth of winter London's Chinese community celebrate their New Year with street processions, much feasting and the traditional good luck dragon.

The Hong Kong Chinese, who have settled in London's Soho, commemorate their New Year with a festival which the British enthusiastically support. The main festival takes place in Soho, where the Chinese community have made certain parts their own – the area is marked by two colourful arches which announce to visitors that this is Chinatown.

Chinese people have been in London for many years, but in the last quarter of a century they have moved from the East End area of Limehouse to the West End, into the streets between Shaftesbury Avenue and Leicester Square. In Chinatown almost every shop and restaurant is Chinese and visitors can sample every kind of Chinese cuisine, from Canton and Pekinese to Szchewan, as well as shop for the ingredients to create the dishes at home. In the Chinese supermarkets rows and rows of cured ducks, sides of dried fish, octopus and seaweed can be seen hanging from rails and the shelves are full of cans and boxes of dried crab, shrimps, ducks' feet and other exotic delicacies, together with the appropriate sauces. There are also shops selling Chinese bric-a-brac such as lamps, ceramics and scrolls, sandals, Chinese books and musical instruments.

During the Chinese New Year celebrations in February this whole area becomes particularly animated. Coloured flags and bunting are strung along the streets and the Chinese set about cleaning their houses, for the New Year is a period of stocktaking and renewal. The purpose of cleaning is to drive out all evil spirits that may have moved into the house during the past year and may have infected the occupants with evil and bad thoughts towards each other. Once evil has been driven out – and sometimes it takes fireworks to ensure that the process is complete – the New Year celebrations can begin.

Everyone goes out onto the streets to greet their friends and neighbours and to watch the brilliantly decorated lions that weave and dance their way through the crowds, while their attendants collect money for charity. The shops contribute money too, but they hang the packets of 'lucky money' just out of reach so that the lions have to leap into the air to reach them. The lions stand for the qualities of energy, courage and benevolence which the Chinese people hope to find in themselves throughout the coming year, and the performance of the lions is a good omen. The colourful beasts are also the ushers of the New Year, which will be named after one of the twelve creatures who give their names to the twelve months of the oriental zodiac. The year will have certain characteristics according to whether it is the Year of the Rat, Fox, Tiger etc. which all Chinese people will try to preserve with patience and discretion.

249

The first gleam of spring arrives with the fragile crocuses that spring up in country woodlands and city parks.

After the ritual lion dance the crowds separate to watch other entertainments, including musical and dancing displays, kung fu and other Chinese skills. First, however, comes the important New Year's Day ritual lunch which takes several hours, running to many courses, and includes symbolic foods which are supposedly good for fertility, business success, longevity, health and all the other good things most people hope for.

The day after New Year is usually spent visiting families and the shrines of ancestors, while the third day is spent at home, for this is the day when it is thought that there is a danger of falling out with friends and relatives. The end of the festival is celebrated by the lighting of lanterns in the streets, on ancestral shrines and in the home – with these symbols of hope still burning, the workaday year is begun.

For Britain, the exotic Chinese New Year has become an easily assimilated festival for its occurrence at the end of February coincides with the feeling that the worst of the weather is now over and that spring will soon be on its way. Perhaps there is an element of wish-fulfilment in the thought, but February does bring out the first crocuses and already, in parks and windowboxes, the first green spears of daffodils and tulips are beginning to show. Soon the celebrations of spring will begin and another busy year of festivals and colourful events will fill the glorious social calendar of Britain.

Calendar of Events

Following is a month-by-month guide to the events and local festivals and celebrations mentioned in this book. Exact dates may change from year to year, and full details of these and the many other events held in Britain during the year can be obtained from the British Tourist Authority Travel Information in London (telephone: 01-730 3400). The BTA can also supply the telephone numbers of the local Tourist Information Centres which form a network throughout Britain.

JANUARY
Epiphany Service.
St. James's Palace, London
London International Boat Show.
Earl's Court Exhibition Centre, London
Whittlesea Straw Bear Festival.
Whittlesey, Cambridgeshire
The Burning of the Clavie.
Burghead, Grampian, Scotland
Burns Night.
Celebrated all over Scotland
Up-Helly-A' Viking Festival.
Lerwick, Shetland, Scotland

FEBRUARY/MARCH
Crufts Dog Show.
Earl's Court Exhibition Centre, London
Jorvik Viking Festival.
York, North Yorkshire
Chinese New Year.
Soho, London
All Horse Plough Match.
Fairhead, near Ballycastle,
County Antrim, Northern Ireland
Cheltenham Gold Cup Meeting.
Prestbury, Cheltenham, Gloucestershire
Oxford v. Cambridge University Boat Race.
Putney to Mortlake,
River Thames, London

SHROVETIDE
Shrovetide Football.
Alnwick, Northumberland; Sedgefield,
Durham; Ashbourne, Derbyshire
Shrove Tuesday Pancake Greaze.
Westminster School, London
Shrove Tuesday Pancake Race.
Olney, Buckinghamshire

EASTER
The Royal Maundy.
Held in a different cathedral each year on
Maundy Thursday
Pace Egg Play.
Midgley, West Yorkshire
Easter Parade.
Battersea Park, London
Hare Pie Scramble.
Hallaton, Leicestershire
Pace Egg Rolling.
Avenham Park, Preston, Lancashire;
Scarborough, North Yorkshire

APRIL
Grand National Meeting.
Aintree, Liverpool, Merseyside
Badminton Horse Trials.
Badminton, Avon
Shakespeare's Birthday.
Stratford-upon-Avon, Warwickshire.
International Clowns Convention.
Bognor Regis, West Sussex
1000 Guineas Stakes.
Newmarket, Suffolk

MAY
Padstow 'Obby 'Oss' Celebrations.
Padstow, Cornwall
Ickwell May Day.
Ickwell Green, Bedford
Royal May Day.
Knutsford, Cheshire
May Morning Celebrations.
Oxford, Oxfordshire
2000 Guineas Stakes.
Newmarket, Suffolk
The Furry Dance.
Helston and Bude, Cornwall
Brighton Festival.
Brighton, East Sussex
Spalding Flower Parade.
Spalding, Lincolnshire
London Marathon.
Blackheath to Westminster Bridge, London
Garland Day.
Abbotsbury, Dorset
Royal Windsor Horse Show.
Home Park, Windsor, Berkshire
Morris Dancing.
Bampton, Oxfordshire
Ayrshire Arts Festival.
Various venues, Ayr, Strathclyde, Scotland
Chelsea Flower Show.
Royal Hospital, Chelsea, London
Founder's Day.
Royal Hospital, Chelsea, London
Well-dressing.
Burton-upon-Trent, Staffordshire;
Wirksworth, Derbyshire
Medieval Jousting.
Start of the spring/summer events at Belvoir
Castle, Belvoir, Leicestershire
Pitlochry Festival Theatre Season
(May–October).
Pitlochry, Tayside, Scotland

Royal Ulster Agricultural Society Annual Show.
Balmoral, Belfast, County Antrim,
Northern Ireland
Bath International Festival.
Bath, Avon
Glyndebourne Festival Opera Season
(May–August).
Glyndebourne, near Lewes, Sussex
Rochester Dickens Festival.
Rochester, Kent
Cheese Rolling.
Randwick, Gloucestershire

ASCENSION DAY
Beating the Bounds.
Oxford, Oxfordshire
Well-dressing.
Tissington, Derbyshire

JUNE
Royal Academy Summer Exhibition
(June to August).
Burlington House, Piccadilly, London
The Derby.
Epsom, Surrey
Appleby Horse Fair.
Appleby, Cumbria
Robert Burns Festival.
Alloway, Ayr, Largs, Irvine and
Kilmarnock, Strathclyde, Scotland
The Flitch Trials (every leap year).
Great Dunmow, Essex
Well-dressing.
Youlgreave and Tideswell, Derbyshire
Common Riding.
Hawick and Selkirk, Borders, Scotland
Aldeburgh Festival of Music and the Arts.
Aldeburgh, Suffolk
Trooping the Colour.
Horse Guards Parade, Whitehall, London
The Garter Ceremony.
Windsor Castle, Windsor, Berkshire
Royal Ascot.
Ascot, Berkshire
Broadstairs Dickens Festival.
Broadstairs, Kent
Lawn Tennis Championships.
Wimbledon, London
Alnwick Fair.
Alnwick, Northumberland

JULY

Rush-bearing.
Ambleside, Cumbria

Henley Royal Regatta.
Henley-on-Thames, Oxfordshire

Cheltenham International Festival of Music.
Cheltenham, Gloucestershire

Llangollen International Musical Eisteddfod.
Llangollen, Clwyd, Wales

Royal International Agricultural Show.
Stoneleigh, Kenilworth, Warwickshire

European Dressage Championship.
Goodwood, West Sussex

Wellington Country Fair.
Stratfield Saye, Hampshire

Great Yorkshire Show.
Harrogate, North Yorkshire

Well-dressing.
Buxton, Derbyshire

Royal Tournament.
Earl's Court Exhibition Centre, London

British Open Golf Championship.
Venue in Scotland changes yearly

Henry Wood Promenade Concerts
(July to September).
Royal Albert Hall, London

Royal Welsh Show.
Llanelwedd, Builth Wells, Powys, Wales

Goodwood Races.
Chichester, West Sussex

Common Riding.
Llangholm, Dumfries and Galloway

Chatsworth Game Fair.
Chatsworth House, near Bakewell, Derbyshire

Yeovilton International Royal Navy Day.
Yeovilton, Somerset

AUGUST

Cowes Week.
Cowes, Isle of Wight

Rush-bearing.
Lauder, Borders, Scotland

Yeovilton International Air Day.
Yeovilton Royal Navy Air Station, near Yeovil, Somerset

Edinburgh Military Tattoo.
Edinburgh Castle, Edinburgh, Lothian, Scotland

Edinburgh International Festival.
Edinburgh, Lothian, Scotland

Battle of the Flowers.
Jersey, Channel Islands

The Burryman.
Queensferry, Lothian, Scotland

West of England Steam Engine Society's Rally.
Tywarnhayle Farm, St. Agnes, Cornwall

Grasmere Sports.
Grasmere, Cumbria

Three Choirs Festival.
Worcester, Hereford or Gloucester Cathedrals

The Old Lammas Fair.
Ballycastle, County Antrim, Northern Ireland

Cowal Highland Gathering.
Dunoon, Strathclyde, Scotland

Portsmouth Navy Days.
Naval Base, Portsmouth, Hampshire

Notting Hill Carnival.
Notting Hill, London

SEPTEMBER

Braemar Royal Highland Gathering.
Braemar, Grampian, Scotland

Ben Nevis Race.
Fort William, Highland, Scotland

English Wine Festival.
The English Wine Centre, Alfriston, East Sussex

Boundary Riding (next in 1990).
Richmond, North Yorkshire

Farnborough Air Show (on alternate years).
Farnborough, Hampshire

Llandrindod Wells Victorian Festival.
Llandrindod Wells, Powys, Wales

Widecombe Fair.
Widecombe-in-the-Moor, Dartmoor, Devon

Burghley Horse Trials.
Burghley, Stamford, Lincolnshire

The Horn Dance.
Abbots Bromley, Staffordshire

Egremont Crab Fair.
Egremont, Cumbria

OCTOBER

Nottingham Goose Fair.
Nottingham, Nottinghamshire

Costermongers' Harvest Festival.
St. Martin-in-the-Fields, Trafalgar Square, London

Mop Fair.
Tewkesbury, Warwickshire

Glenfiddich World Piping Championships.
Blair Castle, Blair Atholl, Tayside, Scotland

Horse of the Year Show.
Wembley Arena, Wembley, London

Tavistock Goose Fair.
Tavistock, Devon

Taunton Carnival and Cider Barrel Race.
Taunton, Somerset

The National Trust Snowdonia Marathon.
Snowdonia, Gwynedd, Wales

NOVEMBER

London to Brighton Veteran Car Rally.
Hyde Park, London to Brighton, East Sussex

Bridgwater Carnival.
Bridgwater, Somerset

Guy Fawkes Festival.
Glastonbury, Somerset

Lewes Bonfire Night.
Lewes, East Sussex

The Lord Mayor's Procession and Show.
City of London, London

Remembrance Sunday.
Whitehall, London

DECEMBER

Royal Smithfield Show.
Earl's Court Exhibition Centre, London

National Cat Club Show.
Olympia, West Kensington, London

Festival of Nine Lessons and Carols.
King's College Chapel, Cambridge, Cambridgeshire

Mumming Plays.
Marshfield, Avon

Sword Dancing.
Flamborough, Humberside

Index

Figures in italics refer to captions

Abbotsbury 37
Abbotsford 114
Abbots Bromley Horn Dance 12, *12*
Aberdeen 182
Abingdon Morris Men 29
Abinger Hammer, 87, *178*
Aboyne Castle 182
Admiralty Arch 67, *213*
Admiralty House 91
Aintree 42, 43, *43*
air shows 147, *147*, 224, *224*
Aldeburgh Music Festival 12, 160–61
Alexandra Palace *215*
Alfriston 160, *192*, 195
All England Lawn Tennis and Croquet
  Club 104, *104*

All Hallows Eve 179
All Horse Plough Match 9, *9*
All Saints Day 179
Alloway 153, *154*
Alnwick 27, 133
Alnwick Fair 133, 135, *135*
Ambleside 12
Angel, Islington *234*
Anglesey 189
Appleby Fair 128, *128*
Ardrossan 180
art 12, 81, 82–3, *82*, *83*
Ascension Day *114*
Ascot *see* Royal Ascot
Ashbourne *11*, 26, 27
'Ashes, The' 110
Askham 132
August Bank Holiday 177

Avebury 128
Avenham Park, Preston 28
Avon, River 71, 115, *115*, *195*
Ayr 9, 153, *154*
Ayr Arts Festival 153
Aythorpe Roding 140

Badminton Horse Trials 45, 48–50, *49*,
  50, 189
bagpipes 12, *180*, 183, 184, *184*, 237,
  239
Bakewell 128, *128*
ballet 233, 234, *234*
Ballochbuie forest 182
Ballycastle 136–8, *136*
Balmoral 180
Balmoral Castle 182, *182*
Balmoral (Northern Ireland) 57, *58*

Bankside, London 6
Banqueting House, Whitehall 213
Barnes Bridge 60
Barrington Court 147
Barton Manor 195
Basildon House 100
Bath 49, 154
Bath Abbey 154, *154*
Bath Festival 154, 156, *156*
Battersea Park 7, *15*, 73
Battle of the Flowers, Jersey 172–3, *172*, *173*
Beachy Head 156, 160
beating the bounds *114*
Beaufort House 73
Beaumaris 189
Beddgelert 188
Bedfordshire 29
Beefeaters *245*
Belgravia 228
Bell's Life 84
Belvoir Castle 53, 54, 55, *55*
Bembridge 101
Ben Nevis 185, *185*, *186*, 187
Berkeley Castle 168
Bess of Hardwick 128, 202, *202*, 203
Betwys-y-Coed 189
Big Ben 67, 210, 221
Billingham International Folklore Festival *135*
Billingsgate fish market 66
Bird Cage Walk, London 21, 67
Birmingham 115
Bishops Waltham 146
Bisley 36
Black Country 115
Black Mountains 209
Black Rock 79
Blackfriars Bridge 66
Blackheath 65
Blair Atholl 184
Blair Castle 180, *183*, *184*, 184
Bloody Assize 207
Bluebell Line 39, *39*
Boat Race, the 11, 59–61, *59*, *60*
Bodmin Moor 36, *124*, 125, 204
Bognor Regis 36, 37, *37*
Bond Street, London 231
Bonfire Night 213–15, *214*, *215*
Bournemouth *173*
Bow Church, London 219
Bowness 133
Box Hill 87, *87*
Boxing Day *236*
Bradford-on-Avon 49
Braemar 180, 182
Braemar Highland Games 180, *180*, 182, *182*
Brecon Beacons 209, *209*
Bridge of Sighs, Cambridge 53
Bridgwater *216*
Brighton 77, 79, 160, 209, 210–11, *210*; Dome 79; International Festival 76, 77, *77*, 79, *79*; Royal Pavilion 79, 210; Theatre Royal 79
Bristol 154, *197*
Britannia Trophy 101
British Academy 82
British Open Golf Championship *110*, 111, 112
Britten, Benjamin 160, *160*, 168
Britten-Pears School of Advanced Musical Studies 161
Broadstairs 173, 174
Brown, 'Capability' 189
Brown Willy *124*
Buckingham Palace 16, *17*, 18, 21, *21*, 67, 82, 213, 221
Buckland Abbey 205, *205*
Buckland Monachorum 205, *206*
Bude 24
Builth Wells 121, *121*, 122, 209
Burford Bridge 87
Burghend 246, *246*

Burghley Horse Trials 189, 192, *192*
Burghley House 189, 192
Burlington House, Piccadilly 82, *82*, 83
Burning of the Clavie 246–7, *246*
Burns, Robert 9, 153–4, 237, *237*, 239
Burns Festival 153–4, *154*
Burns Night 237, *237*, 239
Burryman *137*, 138–9
Burton-upon-Trent 36
Buttermere 133
Buxton 128

Cadbury Hill 150
Cader Idris *188*, 189
Caernarvon 189
Caithness 180
Cam, River 53, *53*
Cambrian Mountains *121*, 209
Cambridge 14, 53, *53*
Cambridge University 59, *59*, 60, *60*, 61, 62, *see also* individual colleges
Cambridgeshire 53
Camelford 34
Camelot 34, 150
Cardigan Bay 189
Carisbrooke Castle 101
carol singing 232, *233*
Carr Taylor 195
Castell Collen 209
Castell Dinas Bran 165, *166*, *166*
cat shows 10, 238
ceilidhs 154, *154*, 161
Cenotaph 213, 221, *221*
Cernian *188*
Ceremony of the Keys 243, 244–5
Changing of the Guard 18, 21, *21*
Channel Islands 172
Charles, Prince of Wales 56, 93, 101, 103
Charles I, King 21, 24, 65, 98, 101, 211, 213
Charles II, King 7, 71, 73, 79, 142, *142*, 168, 207
Charleston 160
Charlie, Bonnie Prince 163, 180, 182
Chatham 177
Chatsworth Game Fair 128, *128*
Chatsworth House, 128, *128*
Cheapside, London 219
Chedworth 48
Cheese Rolling (Randwick) 7
Chelsea, London 60, 71, 73; Bridge 73; Flower Show 10, 73, *73*, 76; Harbour 242; Pensioners 73, *73*; Reach 242; Royal Hospital 10, 71, *71*, 73, *73*
Cheltenham 45, 48, 49, 154
Cheltenham National Hunt 45, *45*, 48
Chichester 146, 147
Chiltern Hills 97, 100
Chinese New Year 248–50, *249*
Chipping Sodbury 49
Chiswick 60, 73
Christmas 227–229, 231–3, *231*, *232*, *233*
Church of England 214
Cirencester 48
Cirencester Park 103
City of London 66, 216, *217*
Civil War 21
Clandon Park 87
Clare College, Cambridge 53
Clarence House 213
Cleopatra's Needle 67
clog dancing 245
Cobham 85
coffee houses 82
Coldstream Guards Band 126
Coliseum 233, 234
College of Arms 96
Colwyn Bay 189
Common Ridings 112–14, *112*
Compton Pauncefoot 147, 150
Conwy 189

Cornwall 34, 124–5, 126
Corpus Christi College, Cambridge 53
Costermongers' Harvest Festival *196*
Cotehele House 205
Cotswold dancing 245
Cotswolds 45, 48, 49
Cottage Rake 48
Coulsdon 210
Covent Garden 233
Cowdray Estate 146
Cowdray Park 103
Cowes Week 100, *100*, 101, *101*
Craigevar Castle 182
Crathes Castle 182
Crathie Church 182
Crewkerne 147
cricket 11–12, 103, *103*, 106–7, *107*, 110–11, 177, 195
Cromwell, Oliver 6, 21, 24, 79, *183*
croquet 106, 177
Crown Jewels 244
Crufts Dog Show 240–42, *240*
Crummock Water 133
Cuckmere Haven *157*
Cuckmere Valley 9
Cullardoch 182
Culloden, battle of *183*
Cup Final Day 11, 63–4, *63*, *64*
Cutty Sark 66, *66*
Cwellyn, Lake 189

Dartmoor *203*, 204, *206*
Davis Cup 106
Dee, River 165, 180, 182
Derby, the 9, 81, 83, 84–5, *84*, *85*, 113
Derbyshire 26, 27, 36, 37
Derwent Water 133
Dickens, Charles 87, 173, *173*, 177
Dickens Festival 173, *177*
Dickens House Museum 177
Didcot Railway Centre 39, 41, *41*
Dingwall 180
dog shows 10, 195, 229, 240–42, *240*
Doncaster racecourse 41–2, *41*, 83
Doom Bar Pirates 32
Dorking 85, 87
Dover House 91
Downing Street, London 213
Dozmary Pool 36, 125
Drake, Sir Francis 205
Drum Castle 182
Drumtochty 180
Dryburgh Abbey 114
Dunmow Flitch 12, 139–40, *139*
Durham 27, 245

Earls' Court Exhibition Centre 227, 239, 240
East Coker 150
East Cowes 101
East Horsley 85
East Meon 146
Easter 24–8
Easter Parade 7, *15*
Easter Sunday 7, 24
Edge Hill 24
Edinburgh 112, 161, 163–4, *163*; Castle 151, *153*, 164; International Festival 12, 151, 161–4, *162*; Military Tattoo 151, *153*, *153*
Edinburgh, Duke of *see* Philip, Prince, Duke of Edinburgh
Edward I, King 17, 189, 197, *199*
Edward II, King 17, 168
Edward III, King 17, 93, 142, 248
Edward IV, King 57
Edward VII, King 84, 91, 97, 101, 172
Edwin 151
Edwinstone 203
Egremont Crab Fair 195, *195*
Eisteddfods 164–6
Elizabeth I, Queen 16, 18, *18*, 121, 189, 195, 214, 217, 219, 244

Elizabeth II, Queen 16, 93, 96, 96, 97, 172, *173*, 211, 213, *213*, 221, *221*
Elizabeth Sutton Place 87
Ellisland 153
Ely Cathedral 18
Embankment, London 67, 73
English National Opera 233
English Wine Centre 195
Ennerdale Water 133
Epiphany 246
Epiphany Service 243, 245
Epsom 84, 85, 87
Epsom Downs 83, *84*, 85, *85*
equestrian events 9, 55–7, 189, 192, *192*
Eskdale 113
Ethelred, St 168
Eton 55
Excalibur 36, 125

Fairhead 9, *9*
Falkland Palace 112
Falmouth 126
Farnborough Air Show 224, *224*
Fastnet Race 242
Fawkes, Guy 213, 214, 215, *215*
Festival of Nine Lessons and Carols 232
Ffestiniog 39
Fiddlers Rally 154
Field, The 106
Fife 112
Finstown 141
Fire of London 219
fireworks 7, 38, 79, *79*, 214, *214*, 215, *215*, 219, 249
Firle Place 160
Firth of Forth *110*
Fishbourne 146
Fitzherbert, Mrs 77, 160
Fitzwilliam Museum, Cambridge 14, 53
Flamborough Sword Dancers 246
Fleet Street, London 219
Flodden, battle of 114
flower festivals 10, *10*, 73, *73*, 76, 79
Flushing 126
football *11*, 24, 27, 63–4, *63*, *64*
Fort William 185, *185*, 187
Fountains Abbey 120
Fownhope 168
Freshwater 101
Friary Court 18
Fulham 60
Furry Dance, Helston 12, 34, 35–6

Gads Hill 177
Game Conservancy Trust 127
Garter Ceremony 9, 57, 93, *93*, 95, 96
George I, King 166
George II, King 90, 98
George III, King 82
George IV, King 55, 77, 79, 96, 160, 244
George V, King 73, 244
Giant's Causeway 137
Gipsy Moth IV 66
Glastonbury 215; Guy Fawkes Festival 215–16; Thorn 215, *216*; Tor 215
Glencoe 180, 185
Gloucester 166
Glynde Place 160
Glyndebourne 12, 156–7, *157*, 160
golf *110*, 111–12, *111*
Goodwood *146*, 147
Gosport 142
Gourock 180
Graham of Claverhouse ('Bonnie Dundee') 184
Grampian Mountains 182, 187
Grand National 42–5, *43*, 48
Grantchester 53–4
Grasmere 12, *13*, 132, 133

Grasmere Games 132, *132*, 133
Great Dunmow 139, *140*
Great Gable 133
Great Glen 185
Great Western Railway 39, *41*
Great Yorkshire Show 118, *119*
Green Man 138
Green Park, London 82
Greenwich 65
Grenadier Guards 93
Greys Court 100
Grimaldi clowns 234, 237
Guernsey 172
Guildford 85, 87
Guildhall, London 217, 219
Gunpowder Plot 214
gurning 195
Gwynne, Nell 73, *73*, 168

Haddon Hall 128
Hallaton 27, *27*
Hallowe'en 179, *179*
Hambledon 147, 195
Hamilton, Lady Emma 87, 146
Hammersmith Bridge 60
Hampstead 107
Hampton Court 104
Hardwick hall 202–3
Hare Pie Scramble 27, *27*
Harrogate 118, *120*
Harvest Festivals 196, *197*
Hatchland 87
Hathaway, Ann 68, 69, 71
Hawick 113
Hay-on-Wye 209
Headingly, Leeds 12
Hebrides 187
Hellvellyn 133
Helston 12, 34, 35–6
Hemingford Abbots 54
Hemingford Grey 54
Hendon 224
Henley Bridge 99
Henley Royal Regatta 11, 60, 97–8, *99*, 103
Henley-on-Thames 60, 97–8
Henry I, King 204, 227
Henry II, King 55, 202
Henry III, King 244
Henry V, King 243
Henry VII, King 142, 211
Henry VIII, King 57, 65, 73, 142, 204, 211, 243, 244
Hereford Cathedral 166, 168
Herm 172
Hermitage Castle 113
High Roding 140
Highgate 107
Highland dancing 114, 184
Highland Games 180, *180*, 182, *182*, 184
Hinton House 147
Hinton St George 147
Hobby Horse, Padstow 7, 32–4
Hogmanay 237
Holyroodhouse, Palace of 161
Honourable Company of Master Mariners 67
Horse Guards 16, 21, *21*, 213
Horse Guards Parade 91, *91*, 93, 221
Horse of the Year Show 224–6, *225*, 226
horse-racing 9, 24, 41–5, 50, *50*, 51, 81, 83, 84–5, *84*, *85*, 96, 97, 102, 114, 147
Hounslow 102
House of Commons 213
House of Lords 213
Household Cavalry 21, 56, *56*, 90, 93, 96, 126, 127, 151, 213, 226
Houses of Parliament 67, 91, 213
Hungerford footbridge 67
hunting 228–9

Huntly House 161
Hurlingham Club 102
Hyde Park, London 16, *17*, 209

ice shows 229
Ickwell 29
Inner Temple 73, 219
International Boat Show 241, 242–3
International Clowns Convention 36, 38, *38*
International Eisteddfod of Wales 164, 165–6, *165*
International Polo Day 103
International World Travel Market 238, 239–40
Invergarry 180
Inverness 185
Island Sailing Club 101
Isle of Dogs 66
Isle of Mull 185
Isle of Wight 100–101, 142
Islington 234

Jack o' the Green 6
Jacobite Rebellion 182
James I, King (VI of Scotland) 151, 153, 214
James II, King 17, 153, 207
James V, King of Scotland 112
jazz 79, 164, 195
Jersey 172–3, *172*, ˜*173*
Jersey Battle of Flowers 172–3, *172*, *173*
Jockey Club 41, 44
John, King 168, 216
Johnson, Dr Samuel 49, 153
Jolablot 248
Jorvik Viking Festival 248, *248*
Joseph of Arimathea 215, *216*
joustling tournaments 9, *9*, 54–5, *55*

Keats, John 87
Kennel Club 241
Kenwood House *81*
Kew 61
Killiecrankie 184
King Arthur's Castle 34
King's College, Cambridge 53, 232
Kirkwall 141
Knaresborough 120
Knox, John 161, *163*
Knutsford 6

Ladbroke 43
Lake District 132–3, *132*
Lamberhurst 195
Lambourn 127
Lancashire 28
Lands End 36
Langholm 112–13, *112*
Langstone 146
Langtry, Lily 83, 233
Lauder 113, 114
Law Courts, London 217, 219
Lawn tennis 104, 106 see also tennis
Leaden Roding 140
Leamington Spa 104
Leander Club 99
Leatherhead 85
Ledbury 168
Leeds Castle 215
Leicestershire 27, *27*, 245
Leith Hall 182
Leith Hill 87
Lerwick 9, 247–8, *247*
Leven, Loch 185
Lewes 214
Lexham Hall 195
Life Guards 17
Limehouse, London 249
Lincoln 41
Lincoln's Inn Theatre 235
Lincolnshire 189

Lincolnshire Handicap 41–2
Linlithgow 138
Little Dunmow 139
Liverpool 43
Livery Companies 217
Lizard 36
Llanberis 186, 187, 189
Llandrindod Festival 208–9, 208
Llandrindod Wells 207–8, 209
Llandudno 189
Llangollen 164, 165–6, 165, 166
Lleyn peninsula 189, 189
Loch Leven Castle 112
Loe Pool 36
London Marathon 64–8, 65, 66, 67
London Wall 217
London Zoo 107
London Zoological Society 107
Lord, Thomas 107, 147
Lord Mayor's Show 179, 216–17, 217, 219, 219
Lords Cricket Ground 12, 106–7, 107, 110, 147
Loseley Hall 87
Lowther Castle 132
Lutyens, Sir Edwin 221, 233
Lydford 206

Macbeth 247
Magdalene College, Cambridge 53
Magna Carta 211, 216
Maid Marion 203
Maidenhead 97
Mall, London 16, 67, 90, 93, 213
Malmesbury 49
Maltings, Snape 160–61
Malvern Hills 168, 168
Manaton 203
Mansfield 202
Mansion House 217, 219
Mapledurham 100
Marconi, Guglielmo 137
Marlborough 127
Marlborough House 213
Marlow 100
Marshfield Mummers 236
Mary, Queen of Scots 112, 113, 128, 153, 183, 203
Mary II, Queen 244
Mary Rose 142
Mary Tudor 6, 214
Marylebone Cricket Club 12, 106, 107, 107, 110
Mathematical Bridge, Cambridge 53
Matlock 128
Maundy ceremony 7, 16–18, 18
Maundy Thursday 24, 243
May Day 6, 28, 32, 33, 36, 79
Maypole 28, 29, 79
Menai Strait 189
Mendip Hills 215
Merlin 127
Michelham Priory 195
Middle Temple 219
Midgely 28
Midhurst 146
Minchinhampton 48
Montacute 147
Mop Fairs 195–6, 195
More, Sir Thomas 73, 244
morris dancing 6, 28, 29, 32, 79, 204, 245
Mortlake 59, 60, 61
Much Marcle 168
Muirfield 110
mummers' plays 234–5, 236
music 7, 12, 79, 81, 81, 154–72

Nantclwyd 104
Nash, Beau 49, 156
Nash, John 79, 160, 233
National Agricultural Centre 117
National Cat Club Show 238, 240

National Gallery, London 233
National Maritime Museum 65
National Sporting Club 50
National Stud 50
National Trust 203
Nativity plays 235, 236
Navy Days 142–3, 142
Nelson, Lord Horatio 49, 67, 87, 142, 142
New Sussex Opera Company 79
New Year 237, 248
New Year's Eve 233
Newbury 127
Newhaven 160
Newmarket 50, 50, 53
Newport 101
Newquay 126
Newstead Abbey 202
North Downs 85, 87, 210, 215
North-West Downs 127
North Yorkshire moors 120
Northumberland 27, 245
Norwich Cathedral 232
Notting Hill Carnival, London 177
Nottingham Goose Fair 12, 197–8, 198, 199, 202

Oaks, The 83, 84
Oban 185
Old Burlington House 82
Old Trafford, Manchester 12
Old Windsor 55
Olde Marine Regatta and Carnival 161
Olney Pancake Race 7, 24, 26
Olympia 238, 239, 240, 242
opera 12, 79, 81, 233, 234
Order of the Garter 93 see also Garter Ceremony
Orkneys 140, 141
Osborne House 100
Ould Lammas Fair 136–8, 136
Ouse, River 160, 248
Outer Hebrides 185
Oval, Kennington 12
Oxford 29, 97, 114
Oxford Street, London 231
Oxford University 59, 60, 60, 62
Oxford v Cambridge University Boat Race 11, 59–61, 59, 60

Pace Egg Rolling 28, 28
Padstow Hobby Horse 7, 32–4, 33
Palace of Westminster 211
Pancake Greaze 26
Pancake Race, Olney 7, 24
Pangbourne 100
pantomimes 234, 235, 237
Parliament 211, 213, 214
Parliament Square, London 67, 213
Peaceheaven 160
Peak District 128
Pearly Kings and Queens 196
Pembroke College, Cambridge 53
Pencerdd 164
Pennines 120–21, 128
Penrith 132
Penzance 36
Pepysian Library, Cambridge 53
Perranporth 126
Peterborough 245
Petworth House 146
Philip, Prince, Duke of Edinburgh 18, 56, 93, 96, 101, 213
Phillips, Mark 49, 50
Piccadilly Circus 63
Pitlochry 80
Plas Newydd 165
Plough Monday 245
ploughing matches 9–10, 141, 141
point-to-point 42
Polesden Lacey 87, 87
polo 102–3, 102

Pony Clubs 226, 226
Portsmouth 100, 142, 142, 146, 147
Poultry, London 217, 219
Praa Sands 36
Preston 28
Prestwick 111
Prince Henry's Room, Fleet Street 219
Prince Regent see George IV, King
Princes in the Tower 244
Princeton 206
Promenade Concerts 168, 170–72, 170
Punch and Judy 177, 208
Putney 59, 60, 60, 61

Queen's College, Cambridge 53, 53
Queen's Hall, London 170
Queen's House 65
Queensferry 138, 139

railways 38–9, 39, 41, 57, 198
Randwick Cheese Rolling 7
Ranelagh Gardens 7, 73
Rathlin 137
Reading 100, 126
Real Tennis 104
Red Devils 224
regattas 11, 79, 97–8, 99
Regent Street, London 231
Regent's Park, London 107
Remembrance Day 179, 219, 221, 221
Rheidol 39
Richard the Lionheart 54, 216
Richard I, King 244
Richard III, King 244
Richmond, Surrey 61
Richmond, Yorkshire 113
Richmond Park 60
Richmond Theatre, Surrey 235
Ripley 85
Ripon 120
Road to the Isles 185
Robert the Bruce 153
Robin Hood 202, 203, 235
Rochester Festival 177
Rock Lodge 195
Rosary School, Hampstead 236
Rosedale 120
Rosedale Abbey 120
Rottingdean 160
Royal Academy Summer Exhibition 12, 82, 83
Royal Agricultural Hall, Islington 241
Royal Agricultural Society of England 116, 116
Royal Albert Hall 168, 170, 170, 171, 172
Royal Almonry 18
Royal and Ancient, St Andrews 111–12, 111
Royal Ascot 81, 96–8, 96, 97, 98, 103
Royal Exchange 217
Royal Family 16, 56, 93, 182, 182
Royal Horticultural Society 73
Royal Maundy ceremony 7, 16–18, 18
Royal Opera House, Covent Garden 233, 234
Royal Scots regiment 153
Royal Show 116–18, 116, 118
Royal Smithfield Show 226–7, 227
Royal Tournament 150–51
Royal Ulster Agricultural Show 57–9, 58
Royal Victoria Memorial 21
Royal Welsh Agricultural Society 121
Royal Welsh Show 121–4, 122
Royal Windsor Horse Show 55–7, 56
Royal Yacht Squadron 101
Rugby Championships 11, 61–3, 61, 62
Rugby School 62
Rush-bearing Festivals 12, 13
Rutland, Duke and Duchess of 53, 54
Rydal Mount 132
Rydal Water 133

Sadler's Wells 234
Sadler's Wells Opera Company 233, 234
St Agnes 125
St Andrews 111–12, *111*
St Bartholomew the Great, church of, London 227
St Bartholomew's Hospital, London 227
St Bride's Church, London 219
St Dunstan's Church, London 219
St George's Chapel, Windsor 93, *93, 95, 96*
St Ives, Cambs 54
St James's Chapel, London 243–4
St James's Church, London 82
St James's Palace 18, 21, 82, 213, 242, 243
St James's Park 21, 91, 243
St John's College, Cambridge 53
St John's Wood, London 107
St Katharine's Dock 66
St Leger 41, *41*, 83
St Magnus the Martyr, church of 66
St Margaret's Hope 140–41, *140*
St Martin in-the-Fields, church of *196*, 233
St Mawes 126
St Pauls's Cathedral 66, 219, *219*
St Paul's School 60
Sandown 101
Sca Fell 133
Scarborough 28
Scots Guards 93
Scott, Sir Walter 114, *163*
Scottish Pipe Band 126
Sealed Knot Society 21, 23, 24
Sedan Chair Race 134, *135*
Sedgefield 27
Selfridges, London *231*
Selkirk 113, 114
Setting the Watch 120
Seven Sisters *157*
Severn, River 168
Shakespeare, William 6, 9, 14, 68, 69, 71, 142, 234
Shakespeare Memorial Theatre 71
Shanklin 101
sheepdog trials 10, 123–4, 128
Sheffield Park 39
Sherwood Forest 202, 203
Shoreham 79
Shottery 68, 71
show jumping 10, 50, 59, 118, 122
Shrove Tuesday 24, 27
Shrovetide *11*, 24, 25, *26*–7
Silbury Hill 127–8
Skye 180, 185
Smithfield 227
Smith's Lawn Championships 103
Snape Maltings 160–61
Snowdon, Mount 187, 188
Snowdonia Marathon *186*, 187–9
Snowdonia National Park 189
Soho, London 249
Solent, the 100, *100*, 101, 142, 146
Somerset *216*
Sonning 100
South Downs 210
South Queensferry *137*, 138
South Ronaldsay 140
Southwell Cathedral *18*
Spalding Flower Festival *10*

spas 48, 49, 77, 85, 87, 120, 121, *121*, 128, 168, 207, 208, 209, 234
'Sphairistike' 106
Staffordshire 36
Stamford 189
State Opening of Parliament 179, 211, *211, 213, 213*
steam rally 125–6, *125, 126*
steeplechasing 9, *42*, 48
Stonehenge 128
Stoneleigh 116, *116*
Stratfield Saye 126, 127, *127*
Stratford-upon-Avon 9, 69, *71*
Stratton, Cornwall 24
Stromness 141
Studley Manor 195
Studley Park 120
Suffolk 160
Sussex Weald 87
sword dancing 245, *246*

Taunton 207
Taunton Barrel Rolling Race and Carnival 206, 207, *207*
Tavistock 204, *204*, 206
Tavistock Goose Fair 12, *203*, 204–5
tennis 12, 103, 104, *104, 105*, 106
Test Matches 11–12, 106, *107*, 110
Tetbury 49
Tewkesbury Fair 195–6, *195*
Thames, River 11, *15*, 59, 60, *60*, 65, 66, 67, 73, 97, 219, 244
theatre 6, 79, 229, 231, 233, 234, 235, 237
Thirlmere 133
Thoresby Hall 203
Three Choirs Festival 12, 166, 168
three-day eventing 9, 50, 189, 192, *192*
Tideswell 36
Tintagel 34
Tissington 36, *37*
Topham family 43
tournaments 9, *9*, 54, 55, *55*, *102*
Tower Bridge 66
Tower of London 21, 66, 243, 244
Town Moor, Doncaster 41
Trafalgar Square, London 67, 82, *196*, 213, 228, 232, 233, *233*
Traitors' Gate 66, 244
Treasury 213
Trick or Treat 179, *179*
Trinity College, Cambridge 53
Trooping the Colour 16, 87, 90–91, *90, 91, 93*
Truro 126
Twelfth Night 245
Two Bridges 206

Ullswater 132, *132*
Up-Helly-A' 247–8, *247*
Uppark 146

Vale of Conwy 189
Vale of Eden 128
Vale of Llangollen 165
Vale of the White Horse 127
Vale of York 120
Vauxhall Gardens 7
Ventnor 101
Veteran Car Run 209–11, *210*
Victoria, Queen 6, 57, 84, 100, *135*, 180, 182, 209, 244
Victoria Embankment, London 66, 219

Victory 142, *142*
Viking festivals 9, 247–8, *247, 248*
vineyards 192, *192*, 195

Wars of the Roses 211
Warwick Castle 23, 115, *115, 116*
Wast Water 133
Watercress Line 39
Waterloo Barracks 244
well dressing 36, *37*
Wellington, Duke of 126, 127, 165, 244
Wellington Park 127
Wellington Show 126–7, *127*, 128
Wells 215
Welsh Guards 93
Welsh National Eisteddfod 164–5, *164*
Wembley Stadium 63, *63*, 64, *64*, 224, *225, 229*
Wemys Castle 112
West Cowes 101
West Meon 147
West of England Steam Rally 125
West Sussex 146–7
Westminster 216, 217, 242; Abbey 17–18, 24, 91, 210; Bridge 67, *67*, 210; Cathedral 24; School 26
Westmoreland wrestling 195
Whale Island 142
Whitehall 21, 91, 213, 221, *221*
Whitehall Palace 21, 213
White's Club 82
Whittington, Dick 217, *219*
Whittlesea Straw Bear Festival 245, *246*
Whittlesey 245
Widecombe Fair *199*, 200–201, 203, 204
Widecombe-in-the-Moor *202*, 203
Wilde, Oscar 73, 83, 100
William III, King 244
William the Conqueror 54, 57, *172*, 211, 243, 244, 248
Wilmington 160
Wimbledon Championship 12, 104, *104, 105*, 106
Wimbledon Common 60
Windermere 133, *133*
Windsor 57, *57*, 97; Castle 9, 21, 55, *55, 57*, 93, *93*; Great Park 57, 97, 102; Home Park 54, 57
Wine festivals 160, 192, 195
Wirksworth 36
Wood, Sir Henry 170, *170*
Worcester Cathedral 166, 168
Wordsworth, William 15, 132, 133, 165
World Piping Championships *183*, 184–5, *184*
Wren, Sir Christopher 53, 57, *57*, 65, 66, 71, 82, 219
wrestling 24, 132, *132*, 195
Wye, River 121, *122*, 168, 209

yachting 100, *100*, 101, *101*, 242
Yeomen of the Guard *18*, 243
Yeovil 147, 150, *150*
Yeovilton International Air Day 147, *147*
York 247, 248, *248*
Yorkshire 28, *28*, 245; Dales 118, 120
Youlgreave 36